T0033361

2ND EDITION

STOCK MARKET 101

FROM **BULL AND BEAR MARKETS** TO **DIVIDENDS, SHARES,** AND **MARGINS**—YOUR ESSENTIAL GUIDE TO THE **STOCK MARKET**

MICHELE CAGAN, CPA

ADAMS MEDIA

NEW YORK LONDON TORONTO SYDNEY NEW DELHI

Adams Media
An Imprint of Simon & Schuster, LLC
100 Technology Center Drive
Stoughton, Massachusetts 02072

Copyright © 2016, 2024 by Simon & Schuster, LLC.

All rights reserved, including the right to reproduce this book or portions thereof in any form whatsoever. For information, address Adams Media Subsidiary Rights Department, 1230 Avenue of the Americas, New York, NY 10020.

This Adams Media hardcover edition May 2024
First Adams Media hardcover edition November 2016

ADAMS MEDIA and colophon are registered trademarks of Simon & Schuster, LLC.

Simon & Schuster: Celebrating 100 Years of Publishing in 2024

For information about special discounts for bulk purchases, please contact Simon & Schuster Special Sales at 1-866-506-1949 or business@simonandschuster.com.

The Simon & Schuster Speakers Bureau can bring authors to your live event.
For more information or to book an event, contact the Simon & Schuster Speakers Bureau at 1-866-248-3049 or visit our website at www.simonspeakers.com.

Manufactured in the United States of America

1 2024

Library of Congress Control Number: 2024931023

ISBN 978-1-5072-2232-4
ISBN 978-1-5072-2233-1 (ebook)

Many of the designations used by manufacturers and sellers to distinguish their products are claimed as trademarks. Where those designations appear in this book and Simon & Schuster, LLC, was aware of a trademark claim, the designations have been printed with initial capital letters.

This publication is designed to provide accurate and authoritative information with regard to the subject matter covered. It is sold with the understanding that the publisher is not engaged in rendering legal, accounting, or other professional advice. If legal advice or other expert assistance is required, the services of a competent professional person should be sought.
—From a *Declaration of Principles* jointly adopted by a Committee of the American Bar Association and a Committee of Publishers and Associations

Contains material adapted from the following title published by Adams Media, an Imprint of Simon & Schuster, LLC: *Stock Market 101* by Michele Cagan, CPA, copyright © 2016, ISBN 978-1-4405-9919-4.

CONTENTS

INTRODUCTION 5

THE STOCK MARKET 7
NYSE 16
NASDAQ 21
THE OTC MARKET 25
FOREIGN EXCHANGES 29
INTERNATIONAL INFLUENCE ON THE US STOCK MARKET 38
BULLS AND BEARS 42
BUBBLES 48
CRASHES 54
PANICS 59
THE SEC 63
ECONOMIC INDICATORS 68
STOCK INDEXES 73
THE DOW 74
S&P 500 78
NASDAQ COMPOSITE 80
NASDAQ 100 81
RUSSELL 2000 83
FT WILSHIRE 5000 85
MARKET CAPITALIZATION 86
MARKET SECTORS 92
OWNERSHIP STATUS 94
COMMON STOCK 104
PREFERRED STOCK 106
STOCK CLASSES 109
BLUE CHIPS 112
VALUE, INCOME, AND GROWTH STOCKS 114
CYCLICAL STOCKS 118
DEFENSIVE STOCKS 119
TECH STOCKS 121
INTERNATIONAL STOCKS 122
PENNY STOCKS 126
MUTUAL FUNDS 128
EXCHANGE-TRADED FUNDS . .133
REITS (REAL ESTATE INVESTMENT TRUSTS) 138
CRYPTOCURRENCY 143
DIVIDENDS 148
STOCK SPLITS 153
MERGERS AND ACQUISITIONS . . 156
HOSTILE TAKEOVERS 163
BUYING AND SELLING 175
EXECUTING STOCK TRADES . .180
STOCKBROKERS 185
IPOS 191
ADVANCED INVESTING TECHNIQUES 194
ANNUAL REPORTS 197
STOCK TABLES 202

TICKER SYMBOLS 204
TICKER TAPE 208
INVESTOR MATH BASICS 211
PAR, BOOK, AND MARKET VALUE. 214
EARNINGS PER SHARE. 217
PRICE-TO-EARNINGS (P/E) RATIO 221
THE PEG RATIO. 224
TOTAL RETURNS 225
FIVE CHARACTERISTICS OF GREAT COMPANIES 227
INVESTOR PSYCHOLOGY 230
BARONS, TITANS, AND TYCOONS 233
FAMOUS AND INFAMOUS INVESTORS. 240
HISTORY'S BIGGEST SCAMS. .256
COMMON SCHEMES 261

INDEX 266

INTRODUCTION

If you've always wanted to tackle the ever-changing world of the stock market, this book is a great first step toward success. From practicing investor psychology to figuring out dividends, learning the basics of stocks can be challenging. In fact, throughout the market's storied history, you'll find cases where investors made billions, or lost everything they owned. However, having the fundamentals of this risk-filled world at your fingertips can make all the difference. By following the advice outlined in this book and learning from mistakes made by investors, you're setting yourself up for financial success.

In *Stock Market 101, 2nd Edition,* you'll find updated information that will help you navigate the ins and outs of Wall Street and achieve your goals in this challenging environment. Here, you'll learn how to:

- Unpack the relationship between value, income, and growth stocks
- Understand the relevance of international stocks
- Recognize key differences between mutual funds and exchange-traded funds
- Get into real estate with REITs (real estate investment trusts)
- Decipher cryptocurrency

With each hands-on lesson in this book, you're closer to stock market literacy. And, in addition, you'll find these detailed entries are accompanied by real-world examples from the stock market like Volkswagen's "Dieselgate" or the 2020 COVID-19 stock market crash, allowing you to stay grounded, and showing more tangible (and extreme) successes or failures. All of this information makes taking the plunge so much easier. While investing in the stock market can seem risky, if you've demonstrated caution and restraint with your investing processes, your investments can create a monetary cushion for years to come.

Ultimately, no matter the amount of money you have to invest or how much you currently know about investing in the stock market, *Stock Market 101, 2nd Edition* will help you on your quest to learn everything you ever wanted to know about stocks and more. So, turn the page and let's begin.

THE STOCK MARKET

Where Fortunes Are Won and Lost Every Day

It's where anyone has a chance to strike it rich or lose everything: The stock market fuels dreams of building great wealth, but can turn suddenly, crushing those hopes and decimating nest eggs.

From the opening bell at 9:30 a.m. Eastern Standard Time to the market's close at 4:00 p.m., the US stock markets never stop moving. The action, though, is nearly silent, a stark contrast to the Wild West excitement that characterized the markets as recently as the turn of this century. Today, the quiet hum of computer screens has replaced the cacophony of shouting traders and the flurry of paper littering the floor.

THE US MARKET IS BORN

When the United States was in its infancy, the founding fathers worked tirelessly to create a nation like no other. In a brilliant move, President George Washington installed Alexander Hamilton as the first secretary of the treasury in 1789. Under his watch, the US stock market was born. Hamilton founded the country's first stock exchange in Philadelphia in 1790, followed shortly after by the New York Stock Exchange in 1792, where the Bank of New York was the first corporate stock traded.

The markets that now make up what is commonly known as the US stock market are the New York Stock Exchange (NYSE) and the National Association of Securities Dealers Automated Quotations (NASDAQ). Many major international cities like London and Tokyo host exchanges as well.

Though the United States still lays claim to the largest stock market in the world, emerging markets around the globe are rapidly adding to the number of publicly traded companies. All around the world, more than 58,000 companies are publicly traded (meaning anyone can own shares, as opposed to privately owned companies, which strictly limit shareholders), with billions of shares changing hands every day. By understanding how the different stock markets work and compete for your investment dollars, you'll be better equipped to succeed in the investing world.

Competition, both domestic and global, continues to make stock transactions more transparent and more accessible to all investors.

Back in the 1990s, it became clear that individual investors were becoming serious players in the world of Wall Street. With the advent of online investing and an aggressive play for smaller investors by the two leading stock markets in the United States, the NYSE and the NASDAQ, buying and selling investments has gotten easier and much less expensive.

When people talk about Wall Street or "The Market," they're generally referring to the secondary trading market, where the vast majority of investors buy and sell stock. But the primary market is where it all begins. The main difference between these two markets is the players involved: In the primary market, large investors are buying shares of stock directly from the issuing company; in the secondary market, investors buy and sell shares from each other.

PRIMARY MARKET

When a privately owned company wants to raise a lot of money, the kind of funding required to help the company grow to its full potential, its owners may turn to an investment banker. Unlike brokers who help facilitate trades on the secondary market, investment bankers guide companies down Wall Street, helping them turn privately owned businesses into publicly traded companies.

This primary market is where stocks are actually created and sold—which is called "floated"—to the public for the first time. The first sale of stock by a company to the public is an initial public offering, or IPO. And though technically these IPO shares are sold to the public, it's not to the general public; rather, these shares are mainly sold to large institutional investors that have the kind of capital the issuing company is trying to raise.

SECONDARY MARKET

Everyday trading takes place on the secondary market, what people think of as the stock market. These trades take place on the major stock exchanges all around the world, such as the NYSE, the NASDAQ, and the London Stock Exchange (LSE).

Here, in the secondary market, trades take place between investors, without the involvement of the issuing companies. For example, if you buy shares in Coca-Cola, you're purchasing those shares from another investor; the Coca-Cola Company itself is not directly involved in the transaction.

WHY STOCKS MAKE SENSE

Though stocks are often perceived as risky investments, over time they've performed better than any other type of security, even better than gold. Over the course of the last 100 years (1923–2023), stocks have returned an average 10.53% annually, while bonds have returned 5.1%, and gold only 0.4%. What's more, this is true the whole world over, not just in the United States. For long-term real returns, you can't beat the stock market.

In the short term, stock returns can be volatile, but that's not unexpected. What most people don't realize, though, is that other securities, even those that are supposed to be safer, suffer that same fate. Bonds, for example, also see wide swings in returns when looked at for short periods.

The highest long-term returns make stocks very attractive to investors and financial planners alike, but they're not the only reason that owning stocks makes sense. With literally thousands of publicly traded companies trading in the United States alone, there's a huge variety of stocks to choose from, making it easy to have a diversified portfolio. With the wealth of easily available information at your fingertips, you can find technical, historical, and analytical data at a moment's notice, helping you keep track of your investments with very little effort.

Then there's the cash benefit: Stocks are among the easiest assets to liquidate, meaning when you need cash, you can get it fast. On top of that, many stock investments, referred to as income stocks, also pay out regular dividends, providing investors with a steady and reliable stream of cash. In fact, many dividend rates are higher than the interest rates on bonds.

That said, the stock market can have nerve-racking swings (where prices move erratically, like a pinball), exciting run-ups (when prices climb ever higher), and devastating downfalls (where prices plummet). Short-term fluctuations are bound to happen, but sticking with stocks for the long haul is still the surest way to see the best returns.

POLITICS AND THE STOCK MARKET

In the midst of an election year, particularly one marked by pronounced uncertainty, the overall market tends to decline.

Once a new president is elected and takes over, the market tends to follow a fairly predictable pattern. Normally, the first year of a first term brings market volatility as the new administration settles in. The second year in office normally brings mild overall gains, followed by stronger returns in the third year; on average, but not always, stock prices tend to increase by about 17% during the third year of a first term. By the second term, returns begin to settle down, though still increase to an average above 10% a year. Then, volatility comes back as the election season gets underway, leading to more shallow returns. Since 1933, average returns in the year following an election have hovered near 6.7%, though occasionally they've dipped down to negative returns.

Presidential term stages aren't the only factors that influence the stock market. Who ends up in the Oval Office has a clear impact as well, most notably along party lines. For example, since 1945, the stock market has done better with Democrats in the White House (according to CNN).

CORPORATE SCANDALS AND THE STOCK MARKET

Crooked CEOs and corporate fraud make for explosive headlines and gripping TV dramas. They also can have definite and lasting effects on stock prices and the stock market as a whole, especially following news footage of fat cat executives being hauled away in handcuffs.

What's more, the fallout from a corporate scandal can fill newscasts and websites for several years, keeping the company's dirty laundry in the public eye and their stock price on the decline, according to a Stanford University study. That study looked at the impact of thirty-eight damaging CEOs, all at the forefront of scandals (including thirteen cases of outright lying, eight cases of sexual impropriety, and six cases of questionable finances) that took place between 2000 and 2015. Though only about half of the executives eventually stepped down or were fired, all of their companies took stock price hits.

While some corporations are permanently damaged or destroyed by scandal, others rise above the fray and thrive. Whether the story comes from the inner workings of the corporation or from a negative external event, the type of scandal (they're not all caused by questionable CEO behavior) and the steps the company takes to fix the problem make all the difference.

- The tainted Tylenol scare of 1982 caused Johnson & Johnson (JNJ) stock to plummet 17% when several deaths were linked to their popular product. By facing the public scrutiny head-on, and dealing with the problem (which, as it turned out, was not caused by anything the company did), the corporation was able to quickly salvage its reputation and watch its stock price rebound in about four months.
- The Exxon Valdez, an oil tanker, crashed into the Bligh Reef on Alaska's Prince William Sound on March 24, 1989, spilling millions of gallons of oil. This environmental catastrophe was blamed overwhelmingly on corporate negligence, and analysts expected ExxonMobil's (XOM) stock to tank. But it didn't. In fact, even

after the corporation was slapped with the biggest fine in history (at that time)—initially $5 billion in punitive damages—its share price barely dipped by about 4%, and rebounded very quickly. That relatively minor reaction came because the tragic spill happened before social media, so people weren't constantly reminded of it. On top of that, the Supreme Court lowered their punitive damages to a measly $507.5 million, a boon to the corporation's bottom line.

- *E. coli* contamination forced the temporary closing of more than forty Chipotle Mexican Grill (CMG) restaurants in 2015, and that drove the company's stock price down. Through the first months of 2016, the stock price struggled, despite the company's commitment to safer food-handling practices. Sales dropped while food safety and legal costs increased, leaving the company with overall losses on the books. The company had to overcome some serious hurdles, and investors remained wary for three years, keeping the stock price nearly $200 per share lower than it was in 2015, a 27% drop. As of November 2023, the stock has regained its footing and has increased to over $2,200 per share.
- The Volkswagen emissions test scandal of 2015, which affected more than 10 million cars worldwide, led CEO Martin Winterkorn to step down as the corporation's stock price lost ground. With continuing recalls, an ever-increasing stack of lawsuits, promised payouts to VW owners, fines and penalties, and restrictions on VW diesel-model sales in the United States, it's no wonder the company posted billion-dollar losses, or that its July 2016 stock price plummeted 48% from the same time in the previous year. Volkswagen AG (VOW3) shares, which trade on the German stock exchange, have been seeing volatile, up-and-down price movement for years. Their response to the scandal greatly impacted share prices, but investors still seemed wary in 2023.

AFTER THE BELL

Just because the markets close each day doesn't mean trading activity has stopped. From after-hours trading (AHT) to news and announcements, investors around the world can get their financial fixes around the clock.

After-hours trading means just what it sounds like: the purchase and sale of stocks outside normal trading hours on the exchanges. In the past, this activity was limited to large institutional investors and the superrich, but now almost anyone can do it, thanks to the ease of electronic trading.

While this sounds like good news all around, AHT comes with some serious cautions. Because fewer people trade after hours than when the exchanges are open, the market is much less liquid, and wider bid-ask spreads (the difference between the highest price that a buyer is willing to pay for an asset and the lowest price for which a seller is willing to sell it) are common, and prices fluctuate more wildly. On the upside, traders can take advantage of breaking news without having to wait for the markets to open the next day.

The Bell

Every trading morning at 9:30 a.m., a bell (like a school bell) is rung to signal the start of the action on the NYSE. Trading stops at precisely 4:00 p.m., at the closing bell.

FINRA

The Financial Industry Regulatory Authority, FINRA, protects US investors by making sure that the entire American securities industry functions honestly and fairly. This is an enormous undertaking. The authority oversees all of the securities firms conducting business in the United States, and presides over all of the dealings that take place between traders, brokers, and investors.

FINRA is a relatively new player in the oversight game. It emerged in 2007 from the combination of two other ruling bodies: the NYSE regulatory committee and the National Association of Securities Dealers (NASD). Their mandate: "To detect and prevent wrongdoing in the US markets."

As of 2023, FINRA manages up to 600 billion transactions every single day, and as a result paints a clear picture of the US financial markets. With its comprehensive oversight, the agency doesn't miss a thing. In fact, thanks to their dedicated vigilance during 2022, FINRA:

- Initiated 743 disciplinary actions against investment firms and brokers
- Imposed $54.5 million in fines
- Sent more than 663 insider trading and fraud cases to the SEC (the US Securities and Exchange Commission)
- Returned $26.2 million of compensation to defrauded investors

While it may seem like FINRA and the SEC do the same thing, they don't. The SEC strives to ensure fairness for individual investors; FINRA oversees brokerage firms and stockbrokers, regulating the industry. Each agency works from a different angle to keep the markets honest. At the end of the day, though, the SEC also oversees FINRA.

NYSE

The Racing Heart of Wall Street

More than 200 years ago, a group of twenty-four Wall Street merchants signed a document called the Buttonwood Agreement. The agreement laid out all the rules for buying and selling shares of public stock, including the price for a trading seat. Their rules, which transformed over time, are the framework for today's rules of trading and the foundation of the New York Stock Exchange (NYSE).

The NYSE, also known to insiders as the Big Board, is home to many prominent industry players like Walmart, Coca-Cola, and McDonald's. Among other requirements for inclusion on the NYSE, a company must have at least 1.1 million publicly traded shares of stock outstanding, with a market value of at least $100 million. It must show aggregate pretax income of at least $11.1 million over the three most recent fiscal years, and have had earnings of at least $2.2 million in the two most recent years.

Actual Seats on the Exchange

Until the Civil War, traders sat in assigned seats and waited. Back then, deals were arranged in a "call market" fashion: Stocks were traded one company at a time, and only once their names were called. That changed after 1871, when shares could be traded at any time and the "seats" were no longer literal. Those seats on the NYSE didn't come cheap, either. The lowest amount paid for a seat, way back in 1871, was $2,750; the highest price paid for a single seat was $4 million paid in December 2005.

Until 2006, traders and brokers had to vie for coveted "seats" on the NYSE, but all that changed when it transformed into a publicly traded corporation. Now, those seats are actually equity memberships, though many still refer to them as seats. What hasn't changed: The same strict regulations govern which professionals may obtain one-year licenses to trade on the exchange, and regulators keep close tabs on their compliance and ethical behavior.

With more than $25 trillion in total market capitalization listed (as of August 2023), the NYSE is the largest stock exchange in the world by market capitalization, or market cap, which is the market value of a company in terms of its outstanding shares. The NYSE holds more than a quarter of the total worldwide equities market. Every day on the NYSE, more than 3.8 billion shares are available for trading.

THE OPEN OUTCRY SYSTEM QUIETS

The long-standing tradition of the open outcry trading system is the one portrayed by movies and TV shows, where we see swarms of traders wildly waving their arms and shouting at the tops of their lungs. That realistic portrayal of the NYSE auction market system (before computers took over), where sellers announce asking prices and buyers put forth bids, shows how the market works: The highest bid gets matched with the lowest ask, and the auction trade is completed. Understanding the ins and outs of the trading floor involves knowing what each player does, particularly customers, brokers, floor traders, and specialists.

A customer contacts a broker with a trade request. The broker connects with the floor trader. A floor trader follows the wishes of the broker and looks for the best bid or ask offer from the specialists. A specialist's job is to make sure the trading traffic flows smoothly by making it easy to trade a particular stock, and most specialists handle somewhere between five and ten stocks on any given day. A specialist is responsible for posting bid and ask prices (or quotes), maintaining an inventory of the stocks (to facilitate trading), and actually executing the trades. Specialists act like matchmakers for bidders and askers, connecting as many as possible. If necessary, they will even buy for and sell from their own supply of shares.

Today, trades on the NYSE are all done electronically. Even so, the NYSE system follows a familiar pattern that remains ingrained in market culture. In today's market:

1. A customer contacts a broker, whether by phone or Internet, and tells the broker what stock he wants to buy or sell.
2. The broker contacts the floor trader with the order.
3. The floor trader brings that request to a specialist in that specific stock.
4. The trade gets written up and executed.

Despite frantic market activity, the trading floor itself is a calm, quiet place, its character forever changed by technology. The shouts of traders have been replaced by the quiet buzz of computers, and the floor seems more like the quiet room in a library than a melee.

EARLY DAYS: THE WHITNEY SCANDAL

Though the exchange is highly respected, it's seen scandal. Perhaps none have been as central as when NYSE president Richard Whitney was charged with embezzlement and sentenced to five to ten years in Sing Sing prison.

From 1930 to 1935, Whitney represented and managed the NYSE. Whitney, a hapless gambler, threw his money after everything from blue chips to penny stocks, incurring losses more often than not. In 1931, for example, his debt reached $2 million. Whitney borrowed from just about everyone he knew to offset those losses, then used the borrowed money to buy even more stock, even as the market collapsed around him.

When he could no longer count on friendly loans, Whitney turned to embezzlement, stealing from customers, the New York Yacht Club (of which he was the treasurer), and even close to $1 million from the NYSE's own Gratuity Fund.

Whitney's crimes were exposed after his term as NYSE president, when an audit uncovered his thieving ways. But something good came out of this stock market scandal: The SEC, then a brand-new government agency, set regulations to protect investors against crimes like his.

HISTORY OF THE NYSE

The NYSE, with the distinction of being the oldest stock exchange in the United States, is housed in a 36,000-square-foot facility in New York City's financial district.

Affected by world events, the exchange has seen its share of heart-stopping ups and downs, some of the biggest occurring in just the last forty years:

- On October 19, 1987, the Dow plummeted 22.61%, the largest one-day percentage drop in history.

- On October 27, 1997, the Dow took a 554-point nosedive, triggering for the first time the NYSE "circuit breaker" rule, created to halt all trading activity when it looks like the market might be headed for a crash.
- After the September 11, 2001, terrorist attacks, the NYSE closed for four days, followed by a Dow drop of 685 points, the largest-ever one-day decline in points at the time.
- On March 16, 2020, the circuit breaker rule was triggered when the S&P 500 plummeted by 7% shortly after the market open due to fears related to the COVID-19 crisis.
- On March 24, 2020, the NYSE saw the Dow climb 2,118 points in a single day, the largest one-day gain in history.

In 2007, the NYSE combined with the European stock exchange Euronext, to form NYSE Euronext, a global milestone for the trading community. This market broke a new record, trading more than 5 billion shares in a single day, on August 15, 2007, when trading volume hit an unprecedented 5,799,792,281 shares.

Not content to rest on its laurels, NYSE Euronext acquired the American Stock Exchange (AMEX) in 2008, and fully integrated trading began in early 2009. That combined exchange offered expanded trading capabilities, including stock options, exchange-traded funds, and other specialized securities.

Then, in 2013, everything changed. After more than 200 years of ruling the financial markets, the NYSE was bought by Intercontinental Exchange (ICE). Though it still operates as it did before the takeover, the NYSE is now just a holding in another company's portfolio. The biggest changes have been technological advancements, which allowed the NYSE to operate fully electronically, without a trading floor, during the COVID-19 crisis.

NASDAQ

The Exchange That Launched 1,000 Tech Companies

It was the first of its kind, operating in a way that hadn't been seen before. For generations, stock markets were real places where traders got together to buy and sell shares face-to-face. Then the NASDAQ opened, and everything changed. Though it wasn't widely recognized at the time, this plucky new-style stock exchange would shift the way markets traded, and vastly improve the speed and accuracy of trades.

When it first launched in February 1971, the NASDAQ hosted only 250 companies. Its first claim to fame: The NASDAQ opened as the first fully electronic stock market in the world. Through the turbulent 1970s, the exchange began to grow, and it became a beacon for young computer-based start-up companies, many of which disappeared as fast as they came on the scene. By the 1980s, computers were gaining ground, and two groundbreaking companies issued IPOs, a powerful indication of what was to come. Those two companies, Apple Inc. (1980) and Microsoft Corporation (1986), changed everything, each eventually becoming (at least for a time) the biggest corporation in the world.

The exchange hit a milestone in 1996, when its trading volume finally exceeded 500 million shares per day. Suddenly, the NYSE wasn't the only exchange hosting successful, respected companies. Now the NASDAQ has grown into a full-fledged stock market, listing about 3,200 corporations, and it's destined to keep growing. Out of all the US stock markets, the NASDAQ (which is now officially known as the NASDAQ Inc.) hosts the most initial public offerings (IPOs), and it is drawing in more companies all the time.

Taking Over

NASDAQ is the largest (by number of companies) and fastest-growing stock exchange in the United States, and it trades more shares in a day than any other US exchange. In September 2023, total daily trading volume topped 1.8 billion shares.

The NASDAQ is attractive to new and growing companies primarily because the listing requirements are less stringent than those of the NSYE, and the costs of listing can be considerably lower. Not surprisingly, you'll find a lot of technology and biotech stocks listed on this exchange, as these types of companies typically fall squarely in the aggressive growth category. In fact, the NASDAQ boasts more than $23 trillion total market value, most of that coming from the technology sector. To catch a glimpse of the companies listed on this exchange, take a look at the NASDAQ Composite, a comprehensive stock index that follows all of the corporations listed there (more on that in the NASDAQ Composite section).

The NASDAQ is a dealer market, which means its securities are traded by dealers through telephone and computer networks as opposed to being facilitated by specialists on a physical exchange floor.

DEALER MARKET

Unlike the auction-style trading floor of the NYSE, the NASDAQ works with more than 600 securities dealers known as market makers. Market makers do just what it sounds like they do: They create a market for securities. They even put up their own capital in order to provide a liquid market for investors, making it easier for them to buy and sell shares.

Though the name seems to imply that market makers are individual traders, most are big investment companies (at least on the NASDAQ). That's how they're able to keep a large supply of stocks on hand that can be sold when orders are placed. There's a lot of overlap in the companies that these market makers keep in inventory, which leads to robust competition. Because the exchange is fully computerized, market makers don't conduct business face-to-face, or even over the phone. All trading on the NASDAQ is done electronically.

These market makers compete against one another to offer the best bid and ask prices (or quotes) over the NASDAQ's complex electronic network, which joins buyers and sellers from all over the world. In fact, market makers must offer firm bid and ask prices, creating what's called the "two-way" market (in FINRA terms). In other words, market makers have to trade shares at the bid and ask prices they have quoted. Between the two amounts is the bid-ask spread, the mathematical difference between the two quotes, and the spot where these market makers can make a lot of money. To level the playing field for investors, market makers are legally required to fill market orders at the best bid or ask price for the customer.

A Deal's a Deal

When a market maker enters a bid or ask price for a particular stock, she has to buy or sell a minimum of 1,000 shares at that published price. After that's accomplished, she can close out that "market," and put in a new price for that stock.

A NASDAQ DEAL

Let's walk through the way a deal on the NASDAQ goes down. It starts with the market maker entering bid and ask prices, say a bid/ask of $461/$464 for a share of Netflix. That means the market maker will buy shares for the bid price of $461 and sell shares at the ask price of $464. The difference between those bid and ask prices is $3 per share, and that represents the market maker's profit, known as the spread.

This looks a little different from the investor's perspective. With those quotes, an investor looking to sell at the current market price would receive $461 per share, while an investor looking to buy would pay $464 per share.

THE OTC MARKET

Murky, Shark-Infested Waters May Hide Buried Treasure

The over-the-counter market, or OTC market, includes securities known as "unlisted stock." This unlisted designation means these stocks are not traded on the traditional stock exchanges like the NYSE or NASDAQ. Instead, securities bought and sold on the OTC are traded by individual broker-dealers, professionals who deal directly with each other via the Internet or by phone.

Buying OTC stocks is very different than buying stocks traded on the major exchanges, in that there is no central exchange for them where buyers and sellers are matched up. Rather, you can only get shares through a market maker, who must actually keep an inventory of shares for sale.

To buy OTC shares, you typically must work through a broker (which can include online broker platforms) who is willing to work with the OTC market. Then your broker has to contact the market maker for the security you want to buy. The market maker will name his ask price, which is the amount he's willing to accept for the shares. To sell OTC shares, the process works the same way: Your broker would contact the market maker to learn his bid (or offering) price.

The process seems simple, but it's fraught with risk. Companies traded on the OTC market are usually too small to be listed on a formal exchange, and reliable information about them can be very hard to find. On top of that, OTC shares are not liquid, so it may be very hard to sell them when you're ready to do so.

PINK MARKET

To be listed on the Pink Market (also called OTC Pink), an unregulated offshoot of the OTC market, all a company must do is fill out a form (specifically, Form 211) and file it with the OTC Compliance Unit. All the form asks for is some current financial information, supplied by the company.

A company would be traded here for a few select reasons. First, the company is very small and can't afford to be listed on a more prestigious exchange. Or, perhaps the company has been kicked off a major exchange due to noncompliance. Or, finally, the company isn't real, and its shares are part of a money-making scam.

Some companies give their market maker access to more detailed financial information, including open access to their accounting books. That makes it easier for the market maker to figure out the right stock price. However, many companies don't. They don't have to share any information with potential investors, and they also don't have to file any reports with the SEC, so investors will have a hard time getting reliable or verifiable information before investing.

Ticker Trivia

The trading information for the smallest OTC stocks used to be printed on pink paper, giving them the name "pink sheets." Those paper trades don't exist anymore, but the name stuck, and those shares trade over the Pink Market.

On top of that, companies trading over the Pink Market are usually very small, and their shares are typically held by only a few people. With such a limited market, it can be very hard for investors to sell their shares when they want to.

So what makes Pink Market stock attractive to investors? For one thing, share prices are usually very low, often less than $1. With that minimal per-share cost, even tiny movements in price can bring sizable returns. For example, say you buy 100 shares of stock in Tiny ABC Inc. for $1 per share, a total investment of $100. A few weeks later, the stock goes up by five cents a share, making your investment worth $105 now. That's a 5% return on your investment. The same price movement on a more expensive stock, say one trading for $10 per share, would be barely noticeable.

The real attraction to Pink Market stocks is possibility—the chance that a tiny company will hit it big. In this age of innovation, where the next major breakthrough could come from one guy with a laptop working from his garage, the prospect of getting in on the ground floor is very enticing. Even if the Pink Market stock never makes it onto a major exchange, it still has the potential to bring enormous returns due to the small initial investment.

OTC Pink uses a tier system to give investors a stronger sense of each company's potential risk factor. The three tiers give investors crucial information with just a glance:

1. The *Limited Information* tier includes companies that aren't quite so forthcoming with current information or have declared bankruptcy.
2. The *Dark/Defunct* tier contains companies that either haven't filed any information within the past six months (indicated by a stop sign symbol) or gray market companies, which have no market maker or market transparency (indicated by an exclamation point).
3. The *Toxic* tier comes with a skull-and-crossbones warning to indicate securities that have been marked as suspicious.

Investors who have the stomach for stocks traded on the pink sheets may need to find a willing broker; not all brokers are agreeable to helping clients buy these high-risk securities. Many of these companies are earnestly trying to grow their businesses and will happily share information with agencies and investors alike. But others are flat-out scams, so beware.

FOREIGN EXCHANGES

It's a Small World After All

When American investors see that stock markets overseas are racking up extraordinary triple-digit returns, they want to dive right in and share the profits. Before 2000, it was practically unheard of for Americans to directly buy stocks on foreign exchanges. In fact, as recently as 2006, it was very difficult to trade shares in non-US markets. Certain online brokerages (including Fidelity) now offer investors the option to sign up for international trading, allowing them online access to a variety of overseas stock markets. Although it's gotten easier, buying and selling stocks internationally is still not as easy as buying on the American exchanges.

For one thing, to buy shares on a foreign exchange you first have to convert your money into the local currency, and changes in currency exchange rates can affect your returns. For another, some world markets have a lot less trading volume than the US markets, and that can make it more difficult to find a buyer when you're ready to sell (or find a seller when you want to buy).

In addition, some brokerage firms will not trade on foreign markets directly. Instead, they offer investors the chance to buy into foreign ETFs (exchange-traded funds), foreign mutual funds, or foreign stocks traded on the American exchanges, called ADRs (American Depositary Receipts).

To counteract those impediments, investors can try to open brokerage accounts in the foreign countries where the stocks they're interested in are traded. For example, to directly buy shares in a company traded on the London Stock Exchange, you can work directly with a British brokerage firm. Keep in mind, though, that stocks you buy on a foreign exchange can only be sold on that same exchange, even if the company is listed on other exchanges.

Why go through all the trouble of investing outside the United States? For one thing, though foreign stocks can be riskier for a wide variety of reasons (e.g., limited information, political instability, shifting foreign exchange rates), they also offer a wealth of opportunity. Some of the largest companies in the world are based outside the United States and are headquartered in up-and-coming economies like Brazil and South Korea. On top of that, foreign economies often move differently than the US economy and each other. So, when the US economy is entering a down cycle, the economy in, say, Hong Kong could be in an upswing.

The Time Difference

When you invest directly in foreign stocks traded on foreign exchanges, time will be an issue. Whether you use an online broker or a brokerage firm in the country where the stocks are traded, purchases and sales can only be made when those markets are open, in local time.

Some of the most prominent stock exchanges outside the United States are the London Stock Exchange (LSE), in England; the Tokyo Stock Exchange (TSE), in Japan; the Shanghai Stock Exchange (SSE), in China; the Stock Exchange of Hong Kong (SEHK), in Hong Kong; Euronext NV (ENX), headquartered in the Netherlands; and the Mexican Stock Exchange, or Mexican Bolsa (MEXBOL, or BMV), in Mexico. Though there are many other stock exchanges worldwide, these exchanges are among the world's largest, and hold the lion's share of market capitalization. Let's take a more in-depth look at some of these exchanges.

LONDON STOCK EXCHANGE

One of the oldest stock exchanges in the world, the London Stock Exchange (LSE) has roots going back to the seventeenth century, when traders met in coffeehouses. In 1973, local exchanges were merged to form what was originally called the Stock Exchange of Great Britain and Ireland, later renamed the London Stock Exchange.

For many years, those exchange members made deals on the trading floor in London. Today, trading on the LSE takes place via computers, processing over a million transactions every day.

The LSE operates in more than 100 countries and offers access to both British and overseas securities to investors around the world. It includes around 1,900 companies from more than 100 nations.

Officially called the Financial Times Actuaries 100 Index, the FTSE (pronounced "footsie") 100 index is the most widely tracked stock market index in the world. Launched in 1984, the FTSE tracks the 100 largest blue chip companies listed on the London exchange, representing more than 80% of the LSE's market capitalization.

Prominent corporations listed on the LSE include GlaxoSmithKline, Unilever, and Barclays.

TOKYO STOCK EXCHANGE

The Tokyo Stock Exchange (TSE) was first opened in 1878, trading precious metals and government bonds. Stocks joined the party in the 1920s. Interrupted by World War II, the exchange reopened in May 1949, and by 1989 (right before the big crash) its total market value topped $4 trillion. Now the exchange lists nearly 3,900 firms, including some of the most successful companies in Japan.

You can track the TSE by watching the Nikkei 225 Stock Average, usually referred to simply as the Nikkei (pronounced "knee-kay"), a stock index that tracks the ups and downs of the Japanese stock market. It includes 225 blue chip stocks, all headquartered in Japan. The Nikkei is like the S&P 500 Index in the United States, which tracks the share price activity of 500 of the largest corporations on the market. Another way to gauge the Japanese market is with the TOPIX (Tokyo Stock Price Index). TOPIX, which launched in 1968, tracks primarily large-cap stocks (stocks with market capitalization of at least $10 billion). It includes around 2,000 stocks in thirty-three categories.

Unlike most other major exchanges, the TSE has two trading sessions per day. The morning session, called "zenba," is open from 9:00 a.m. to 11:30 a.m.; the afternoon session, called "goba," runs from 12:30 p.m. to 3:00 p.m. Stocks listed on the TSE trade in 1,000-share blocks, and virtually all trades are executed electronically.

The TSE has a tumultuous history. In 1980, the Nikkei was plodding along at 6,536, but then Japanese stocks soared. By December of 1989, the index had nearly sextupled to 38,916. But in the 1990s, fortune ran the other way, and the Nikkei (along with the TOPIX) took a nosedive. In March 2003, the index plunged below 8,000, and continued to follow a roller-coaster-like path over the next decade. In the first half of 2016, the Nikkei bounced around between 15,000 and 17,000. After hovering near 20,000 for a few years, it started to trend up toward the end of 2020. The index hit its most recent high of 33,772 in July 2023. To limit market volatility, the TSE halts major declines through circuit breaker rules, like those used on the NYSE.

Companies listed on the TSE include big names like Sony, Toyota, and Nintendo.

SHANGHAI STOCK EXCHANGE

Originally opened in the 1860s, the Shanghai Stock Exchange (SSE) was shut down by the Communist Party in 1949. In 1990, the exchange opened again, ushering in a new age for the Chinese economy, one heralded by wild swings, with both market run-ups and crashes.

Unlike other stock exchanges around the world, the SSE operates as a nonprofit organization. It's administered by the CSRC (China Securities Regulatory Commission) and is prone to excessive government oversight. Most of the major companies listed on this exchange used to be state-run companies, including insurance companies and banks. To qualify for listing on the SSE, a company has to be in business and earn profits for at least three years.

The SSE, which is the largest stock exchange operating in China, lists two different types of shares: A shares and B shares. A shares are quoted only in Chinese currency, the yuan. They represent stock in companies based on the Chinese mainland. Until fairly recently, only citizens of mainland China could buy A shares. However, approved foreign investors, designated as QFII (qualified foreign institutional investors) are allowed to purchase them through a special highly regulated system. B shares are open to both foreign and domestic investors, and these shares are quoted in other currencies, like US dollars. Every stock on the SSE trades in both A and B shares.

The main index tracking the Shanghai Stock Exchange is the SSE Composite. This measure is expected to mirror the overall Chinese economy as more state-run companies go public. In 2015, the SSE cycled through majestic highs and painful lows, displaying extreme volatility despite focused government intervention. One reason for those very wide swings was the extremely high proportion of margin trading (when investors borrow against their holdings to buy shares on credit), which involved trillions of yuan. Another reason was the heavy hand of the Chinese government, which exercised its power even as it attempted to offer freer access to foreign institutional investors.

Companies listed on the Shanghai Stock Exchange include Air China, Bank of China, PetroChina, and Tsingtao Brewery. Though some inroads have been made that allow certain foreign investors to buy Chinese stocks, individual foreign investors can more easily invest in these shares using the Stock Exchange of Hong Kong.

STOCK EXCHANGE OF HONG KONG

The Stock Exchange of Hong Kong (SEHK) was established in 1891. Today, the exchange is primarily driven by the country's highly respected and sophisticated financial services industry. Hong Kong has an intimate relationship and trading partnership with China; its exports to that country alone top $350 billion annually, which amounts to nearly 60% of Hong Kong's total exports. The exchange mimics that pattern, with Chinese companies making up more than half of the stocks trading there.

Hong Kong operates as a "special administrative region" created by the central Chinese government to allow the small nation to operate basically the same way it had under the former British rule. For investors, this distinction is crucial, because the Stock Exchange of Hong Kong operates with autonomy in a capitalist country that is governed by a limited democracy (as opposed to China's communist government and socialist economy).

During the late 1990s, this exchange was able to start listing H-shares of large Chinese state-owned companies (the H-share designation simply indicates Chinese stocks traded on the Stock Exchange of Hong Kong, in Hong Kong dollars). This is actually the largest market for Chinese equity securities. Today, the stock of more than 1,400 companies based on mainland China can be traded on the Hong Kong exchange.

The most important index connected to the Hong Kong exchange is known as the Hang Seng. This market cap-weighted index includes the seventy-three biggest corporations traded on the exchange.

Companies trading on the Stock Exchange of Hong Kong include Bank of East Asia, Air China, and Alibaba.

EURONEXT

Headquartered in the Netherlands, Euronext NV (ENX) is a cross-border exchange, and the first Pan-European securities exchange. Euronext was born in 2000 by merging the Paris, Brussels, and Amsterdam exchanges. Then in 2002, the Portuguese stock exchange was added, followed later by a London securities exchange (but not the London Stock Exchange).

In April 2007, Euronext merged with the NYSE Group to form NYSE Euronext. And by 2008, the combined exchange listed almost 4,000 securities with a total market capitalization of more than $30 trillion.

When Intercontinental Exchange (ICE) bought NYSE Euronext in 2013, the two powerhouses were split once again. Still, Euronext remains one of the largest exchanges in the world. In June 2014, Euronext launched its own IPO, and once again became a stand-alone entity. It was joined by the Irish Stock Exchange in 2018 and by the Borsa Italiana in 2021.

The Euronext exchange system opened up the European stock market, allowing companies to list their securities in multiple markets that fall under a single umbrella. For example, a stock listed on the Euronext Paris exchange can also list on the Euronext Amsterdam exchange. To further facilitate trading, they use the euro as the primary trading currency.

Companies traded on the Euronext exchanges include Air France–KLM, Coca-Cola European, and L'Oréal.

MEXICAN STOCK EXCHANGE (MEXICAN BOLSA)

The Mexican Stock Exchange, known as la Bolsa Mexicana de Valores (BMV), is the second-largest Latin American exchange. Headquartered in Mexico City, it is the primary securities exchange in Mexico. The newer and more tech-heavy BIVA (Bolsa Institucional de Valores) is growing quickly, but doesn't have the heavyweight power of the BMV yet.

Considered an emerging market, the Mexican economy has been going strong and is predicted to stay on the move upward. Its forward progress continued, though slowed, even during the worldwide recession that characterized the early 2010s. Mexico is among the top ten oil-producing nations in the world, and even with volatile and low crude oil prices, the country has been able to maintain its economic growth.

When it comes to stock market performance, there are two ways to monitor the Mexican market: the MEXBOL IPC Index, which includes a wide range of companies trading on the Mexican stock exchange, and the INMEX index, which tracks the twenty (or so) companies with the largest market capitalization. Foreign investors should factor in the country's gross domestic product (GDP) when considering investments in any securities listed on the Mexican Bolsa. As agriculture contributes greatly to the GDP, paying attention to that economic sector offers additional insights into the company's overall economic health.

The future of Mexican industry, though, seems to be in manufacturing. The country has rapidly risen to superstar heights in this arena, largely due to free trade agreements and relatively low labor costs.

Companies traded on the Mexican Stock Exchange that American investors may be familiar with include Walmart de Mexico (WMMVY) and Coca-Cola FEMSA (KOF), which is the world's biggest Coca-Cola bottler.

INTERNATIONAL INFLUENCE ON THE US STOCK MARKET

The Butterfly Effect

War, health crises, economic fluctuations, and natural disasters—all of these global events have a large (and sometimes lasting) impact on the US economy and the US stock market. That's how the butterfly effect—a theory explaining how small causes bring large and sometimes unexpected effects—hits the world of finance.

When exports and international sales drop off, the stock market reacts. When oil prices plummet or skyrocket, American corporations see the impact in their stock prices. As the world shrinks, thanks to advancements in communications technologies and international trade deals (like the United States-Mexico-Canada Agreement, USMCA), events in other countries affect the US stock market more than ever before.

Multinational corporations (MNCs) drive much of this international effect. These companies have vast overseas operations that get directly impacted by international events. For example, a US corporation with manufacturing plants in Pakistan could have its operations disrupted by massive flooding. What affects the host country also affects any American corporations with holdings there.

International trading also affects US stock prices. US shares trade on markets all around the world. Due to time differences, there's always a market open somewhere. Because of that, US stocks can be traded twenty-four hours a day, seven days a week, and that has a clear influence on US stock prices.

MULTINATIONAL CORPORATIONS

Multinational corporations (MNCs) are exactly what they sound like: companies that have operations running in more than one country. Based in a home country, these huge enterprises keep factories, shops, plants, warehouses, and offices in multiple nations. That all adds a lot of complications to their corporate structure.

Since every country has its own set of laws, customs, and regulations, a company operating in more than one country needs to bring in teams of lawyers and managers to make sure they're correctly and properly following local rules. As laws everywhere are subject to change any time, multinational corporations have to pay close attention to events in the nations where they have operations and adapt as necessary. At the same time, anything from political instability to cultural sensitivities can affect MNC operations and profits.

MNCs in America

In addition to American corporations having operations in other countries, many foreign corporations maintain offices or plants in the United States. Examples include Unilever, Honda, and GlaxoSmithKline.

More than 700 American corporations maintain overseas operations, companies like Johnson & Johnson, Disney, and Amazon. This setup gives American investors the chance to invest in overseas operations through companies headquartered in the United States. In fact, many US-based companies bring in more than half of their revenues from their foreign business activities.

From an investor's standpoint, this has both benefits and drawbacks. Benefits include things like access to larger markets and tax advantages, both of which may have an immense impact on a company's profitability. One of the important drawbacks is political risk: the chance that a country in which the corporation operates will undergo political or economic changes that have a negative impact on the MNC's profits. Political risk encompasses all manner of issues, from government coups to added financial restrictions to corruption, and any of these can attack a corporation's bottom line.

GLOBAL MARKETPLACE

Whether or not American companies maintain foreign offices or manufacturing plants, they still can participate in the global marketplace. Throughout the world, people gobble up new (at least new to them) American products as fast as corporations can export them. That's why you can visit a Disney theme park in Paris or Tokyo, or buy a Starbucks grande skim latte in more than eighty countries around the world, from Brazil to Vietnam to Indonesia. As American corporations enter new markets and global sales increase, stock prices can rise right along with them.

At the same time, recessions, depressions, and slowdowns in overseas economies now have increasing impact on US companies. For example, economic turmoil in China led to a drop in the share prices of many corporations including Apple, Qualcomm (a semiconductor manufacturer), and Intel. Corporations with operations in China or that rely on Chinese consumers for a substantial portion of their sales have seen a clear negative impact on their business and stock value.

A CLOSER LOOK AT CHINA'S IMPACT

As the second-largest economy in the world, China, with its voracious appetite for raw materials and other commodities, has an enormous impact on other countries and their stock markets, and the United States is no exception.

For example, when the standard of living in China began to dramatically increase, their hunger for Western products became ravenous. Demand for everything from cars to movies to iPhones created a huge new market for American companies. This fundamental shift marked a permanent change for the global economy; once people live through changes like this, it affects their spending habits going forward.

But when the economy of this giant nation weakens, as it did beginning in 2019 with the start of the COVID-19 pandemic, the rest of the world starts to get nervous. Once pandemic restrictions lifted, the Chinese economy surged briefly. But underlying issues like high youth unemployment are dragging the country back down. And because China is one of the United States' primary trading partners, accounting for around 11% of total trade including $10 billion of American exports every month, a slowing Chinese economy signals a potential slowdown for the US economy as well. Corporations that sell products and services to the Chinese market will see those sales drop dramatically, causing a negative impact on their bottom lines and their stock prices.

BULLS AND BEARS

There's a Reason the Stock Market's a Zoo

The drama of stock market activity makes headlines every day. In many of those headlines, you'll see one of two iconic words: "bull" and "bear." One of those words excites investors and spurs rallies, and the other invites fear and caution, and leads nervous investors to cash out. In Wall Street lingo, bulls represent markets on the rise, and bears signify market slowdowns.

Whether the market is characterized as "bull" or "bear" depends mainly on the prevailing direction of stock prices, but that is not the only factor in play. Other issues that contribute to bull and bear markets may include investor emotions, economic ups and downs, supply and demand, and global conditions.

What defines a bull or bear market is time. Long-term market performance determines which animal defines the market, rather than quick spikes or dips that last only a few days or weeks.

SECULAR MARKETS

A market cycle that lasts for many years is called a secular market, regardless of whether it's operating in bull or bear mode. Secular markets last anywhere from ten to thirty years, often brought on by demographic shifts (like the rolling retirement of the baby boomers, where an estimated 10,000 will retire every day), major changes in technology (like AI and biometrics), and significant global events (like wars, climate disasters, and pandemics). In a secular bull market, investors will see above-average returns. In a secular bear market, returns will fall below average.

Ticker Trivia

During a secular market, investor sentiment can temporarily sway in the opposite direction, but will then swing back toward the predominant pattern. This brief interruption does not change the characterization of the secular market trend.

Secular bull markets are associated with record highs, extreme investor confidence, and market bubbles. Secular bear markets are characterized by fearful investors, reduced investing and increased savings, undervalued stocks, and record low stock prices.

Since the crash of 1929, the US stock market has experienced both types of secular markets.

From 1929 through 1949, investors remained wary. With minimal activity, that secular bear market brought minimal returns to those still investing. Suddenly, sentiment shifted and market activity picked up.

In 1950, the market changed course. This launched the longest secular bull market in American history, which finally came to an end in 1968. Though the market did see some short-term downturns during that eighteen-year period, returns averaged 11% over that time span.

The war in Vietnam, inflation, global upheaval, high interest rates, and stagflation (a time of slow market growth and high unemployment accompanied by high inflation) marked the next secular bear market, which ran from 1968 through 1982. Those brave enough to invest in the stock market were rewarded with disappointingly low returns.

In 1982, though, the market took a turn toward the bull. With the Dow returning, on average, nearly 17% annually during this bull market, investors were flying high. Interest rates were down, but corporate profits were soaring, and so were their share prices. This exuberant market lasted until 2000, when the dot-com bubble burst.

When the market crashed in 2000 following the implosion of the dot-com bubble, it set off a secular bear market that resulted in crippling losses. The NASDAQ Composite index, comprised primarily of tech stocks, saw a devastating 78% drop in value. And the average annual rate of return on stock investments during this eight-year bear market, -6.2%, still makes investors shudder.

Some analysts believe that 2009 marked the beginning of the next bull market; others say it didn't truly kick in until 2013. That lasted until February 2020, and at 132 months it was the longest bull market in US history. During that bull run, the Dow saw higher than average positive returns—including several record-breaking highs.

BULL MARKET

Bull markets don't last forever, though it may feel that way in the middle of one. During a bull market, investors expect that stock prices will continue to go up. That can lead to more risky buying behavior, as investors look to reap "surefire" rewards.

Americans have seen several bull markets since World War II. The first began in 1950 and lasted through 1964, and the markets increased by a total 908.5%. The next great bull run began in 1986 and lasted through 2000, breaking one record after another as the Dow and the NASDAQ hit all-time highs again and again. The NASDAQ really soared during this great bull market, shooting up 185%

between November 1997 and March 2000...a period when the Dow increased 40%. Since 2000, shareholders have enjoyed five roaring bull markets, the longest running from 2009 through 2020 with a total increase topping 400%.

The Dow Sets New Records

Back in 1982, the Dow Jones Industrial Average (a calculated index based on the value of a basket of stocks) first broke 1,000. By March 1999, the Dow hit a jaw-dropping 10,000 followed by a record close of 11,722.98 on January 14, 2000. Fast-forward to 2017, when the Dow finally crossed 20,000, waiting just a few years to cross 30,000 in 2020. The Dow's all-time high (so far!) of 36,952.65 was set on January 4, 2022.

These market highs continued to come despite economic catastrophes like the Asian market crisis of 1997 and the COVID-19 pandemic of 2020–2023. During that 1997 crisis, US Federal Reserve Chairman Alan Greenspan uttered his seminal phrase, "irrational exuberance." These cautionary words fell right in the middle of this bull market and would ultimately prove true after the dot-com bubble burst in March 2000, ending that bull market.

After a couple of years on the downside, the US stock market rebounded starting in October 2002. On October 9, 2002, the Dow was at a new low of 7,286. That nearly doubled in just five short years, when the Dow closed at 14,165 on October 9, 2007.

From 2009 to 2020, the United States enjoyed another bull market, characterized by consistent growth, huge increases in the Dow, and more record highs. That run was killed off by COVID-19 in January 2020, despite surviving a trade war, Brexit, the Iraqi civil war, and other potential market tankers. The market rallied and rebounded quickly into a new bull run from March 2020 to January 2022.

The post-pandemic recovery bull market kicked in during October 2022. As of September 2023, the US was still in the middle of this bull run. How long it will last is anyone's guess.

BEAR MARKET

In a bear market, stock prices fall steadily for a sustained period of time. The technical definition of a bear market is at least a 20% decline in any of the major market indexes (like the Dow or the NASDAQ Composite) that lasts for at least sixty days.

That downward trend leads most investors to believe prices will continue to fall for the long haul, so they begin to sell stocks rather than buy stocks. Others, a much smaller group, use bear markets as opportunities to go bargain shopping, scooping up shares of solid companies at depressed prices in the hope that they'll eventually rebound.

Generally, though, increased sales coupled with decreased purchases drive stock prices down further, perpetuating the bear market. Over the long term, this can affect the corporations themselves, possibly leading to lower profits, and even losses and layoffs. Not surprisingly, bear markets are closely linked with weak economies.

Since 1929, the United States has weathered more than twenty-five bear markets. The average loss hovered around 35%, and they lasted, on average, for less than one year each. Some, of course, have been much worse than that, such as the extended bear market that dragged from 2000 to 2002, where we saw a nearly 50% decline in market value. And on the heels of the housing bubble burst in 2007, a seventeen-month bear market resulted in a 56% decline in the S&P 500.

The US has experienced two more bear markets since then. The first lasted just a month, from February to March 2020, when the pandemic was just beginning and uncertainty marked everything. The most recent bear market ran from January 2022 to October 2022, resulting in a 25% decline in the S&P 500.

CIRCUIT BREAKERS

After the disturbing downturns in 1987 and 1989, the NYSE put "circuit breaker" rules in place to stem massive declines before they can snowball into crashes. The latest version of these rules, approved by the SEC and implemented in 2013, calls for trading halts based on very specific events affecting the S&P 500 Index (a measure of the biggest corporations trading on the stock market).

- A Level 1 halt kicks in when the S&P 500 drops by 7% before 3:25 p.m. on a trading day. A Level 1 halt lasts for fifteen minutes.
- A Level 2 halt comes into play with a 13% decline of the S&P 500, again if the drop occurs before 3:25 p.m. It also lasts for fifteen minutes.
- Level 1 and Level 2 halts can only happen once a day each, but a Level 1 halt can be followed by a Level 2 halt if the index declines further once trading resumes.
- A Level 3 halt is the most serious; it suspends trading for the rest of the day. That happens when the S&P 500 decreases by 20% at any time during the trading day.

Those Level 1 circuit breakers kicked in four times in 2020: on March 9, March 12, March 16, and March 18 when COVID-19 fears led to massive sell-offs.

BUBBLES

Don't Pop the Champagne Just Yet

When it comes to the economy, bubbles grow to an unsustainable size and then burst. They start out as pockets of swift expansion and prices soar when everyone wants in, then the expansion suddenly tails off, and prices plummet during a panicked frenzy of selling. When a bubble bursts, it sometimes snowballs into a full market crash.

These bubbles can form in the overall economy, or they can appear in portions of it, from entire markets to market sectors and all the way down to individual securities. What they all have in common is asset prices that are significantly higher than their true worth. Financial experts coined the phrase "asset price bubble" to describe the phenomenon.

Though seasoned analysts may be able to spot a bubble from the inside, these economic events are often identified only after the bubble has popped.

BUILDING A BUBBLE

Though the core of a bubble comes from overinflated asset prices with no basis in reality, the events that spur the irrational price hikes are very real. Bubbles can be set off by things like shifting interest rates, free-flowing credit, and new innovative developments in technology. Once people start to catch the new fever, the bubble begins its tenuous growth, and prices take baby steps upward.

Prices begin to gather momentum as more people jump on the bandwagon. Media coverage increases, which draws in even more excited participants hoping to get in on this strike-it-rich opportunity.

High on the quickly climbing prices, investors throw caution to the wind and enthusiastically pour more money into the mix, sending prices to exorbitant levels, far above what the actual underlying assets are worth. With market values out of control, traders, advisors, and talking heads cook up reasons to justify continued investment.

As prices reach their tipping point, smart investors realize it's time to get out and they try to clear profits before everyone else catches on. But when markets act in irrational ways, it's virtually impossible to make a clean getaway. All it takes is the tiniest pin to pop a bubble, immediately and forever halting its expansion, and setting off its inevitable unraveling.

Now mass panic sets in. The bubble bursts as prices plummet even faster than they rose. Investors desperately try to sell off their overpriced assets before they're fully worthless. With more sellers than buyers, prices hit rock bottom. Individual and institutional investors, whole markets, even whole economies can collapse once the bubble has popped.

A Return to Reality

Despite the fact that fortunes get decimated when asset price bubbles burst, a market correction also brings balance back to the system. In other words, prices return to realistic levels that reflect the intrinsic value of the assets.

THE NEXT BUBBLE?

Investment and economic analysts attempt to forecast the next bubble before it blows up, and they also try to pinpoint the moment right before the burst. While some of them are likely to be right, in truth their predictions can be as much guesswork as foresight. Realistically, bubbles are usually defined only after they've popped, meaning that any investment opportunities have already been lost. But that doesn't mean industry insiders can't pick up on signs that market fluctuations are more than just normal movements.

Not all gains in asset prices are unrealistic. Sometimes value truly increases, even in the midst of investor excitement. As for coming out on the right side of bubble timing, it's as likely as winning the lottery: A few very lucky people may get it right, but most investors won't end up hitting it big. How high prices will rise, how quickly they'll inflate, and how long the bubble will last are all highly unpredictable events. But despite the tumultuous rise and fall of stock prices during a bubble, over time, it still pays to participate in the stock market.

So, what's coming next? Analysts are talking about an "everything" bubble, where prices for anything from houses to groceries to healthcare costs to cryptocurrencies surge out of control. At the same time, debt bubbles may threaten the market; think student loans and medical debt, both hitting alarming levels. Around 45 million Americans have a collective $1.78 trillion in student loan debt. More than 100 million Americans live with medical debt, with 61% of them owing at least $1,000. Those debt burdens can lead to significant shifts in the overall economy and the stock market.

DOT-COM BUBBLE

Picture this: The Internet was just gaining momentum. Personal computers had just become a part of everyday life. It was the 1990s, and the technology was so new that no one could predict the ways it would change our world. At the time, the innovations were intoxicating, and so eager investors wanted in. The rush to profit from these innovations spurred the unfortunate creation of the ill-fated dot-com bubble.

The excitement over dot-com companies grew, and share prices increased accordingly. Most of these new dot-com stocks showed up on the NASDAQ, and the value of the exchange grew five times over in just five years.

During that time, IPOs emerged like ants at a picnic. They commanded huge prices from day one, and some of them saw their share prices gain 100% on that very first day. Hundreds of those companies, almost as soon as they went public, garnered billion-dollar valuations. But most of them were not worth even close to what investors were willing to pony up.

Suddenly, some of the biggest tech companies of the time (like Dell) started to sell shares of their own stock, and investors began to get very nervous, selling off their tech holdings in a panic. Without the constant inflow of capital, most of those "pop-up" dot-com companies went under and their shares became worthless. And, just like that, billions of investors' dollars simply disappeared.

HOUSING BUBBLE

Newspaper headlines contained words like "crisis" and "collapse" and "bailout," and investors began to panic. In the fall of 2008, the major financial markets in the United States lost nearly a third of their value. As the subprime mortgage fiasco unfolded, it dragged the country's economy down with it. Though the US housing bubble wasn't directly tied to the stock market, its collapse did have a huge impact on stock market behavior.

The story of one of the worst financial crises in American history started before the turn of the millennium, back in 1999. The economy was humming along, and the real estate market was booming. Everyone wanted to buy houses, but not everyone had good enough credit to qualify for mortgages. Until, that is, subprime lending to high-risk borrowers became the new standard.

With horrible credit history, limited income prospects, and minimal (if any) savings to fund a down payment, people were nonetheless getting mortgages from greedy predatory lenders. Even worse, those mortgages came with some pretty nasty twists and intricacies that many new borrowers did not understand. The biggest problem: adjustable rate mortgages, or ARMs, where both the interest rates and payments changed periodically, almost always getting bigger.

While the housing market was flying high, these risky loans seemed risk-free. Borrowers appeared to have equity in their homes because the houses were suddenly worth more. That situation was about to change, but not before a lot of investment banks and investors bet big on a new fad known as mortgage-backed securities (MBS). Basically, an MBS is a bond backed by mortgages, and bondholders get paid as mortgage payments come in. As long as people are paying their mortgages, these securities work.

When interest rates on ARMs reset and payments increased, suddenly people couldn't afford to make their monthly mortgage payments and defaulted on their loans. At the same time, home values plummeted.

The housing bubble had burst. Foreclosures became commonplace, and personal bankruptcy rates skyrocketed. And without incoming mortgage payments to prop them up, the MBS market collapsed and took recklessly irresponsible major investment banks down with it.

Those infamous bank failures on top of the distressed mortgage and housing industries dragged the country into a recession in the winter of 2007, and the stock market dropped along with it. By mid-2008, the Dow Jones Industrial Average dropped to a two-year low, and kept falling. As investors pulled their money out of the stock market in a panic, share prices hit devastating lows.

CRYPTO BUBBLE

Cryptocurrencies, like Bitcoin and Ethereum, hit the street quietly at first, but quickly came to be on "hot lists" all over the world. In an attempt to go more mainstream, crypto companies began advertising everywhere from bus benches to Super Bowl ads. And it worked. People began buying and prices began soaring, hitting all-time highs with no substance to back that up.

Then in 2022, inflation hit hard and the Federal Reserve started bumping up interest rates to fight it. The crypto companies expected their "coins" would act like inflation hedges, similar to gold, and the prices would hold steady or climb even higher. The reality: Crypto prices began to fall, and kept falling. Some crypto companies, like FTX, ended up declaring bankruptcy. Scams and fraud were uncovered throughout the industry. Hackers stole nearly $4 billion from the crypto market in 2022 alone. And even the most famous cryptocurrency, Bitcoin, lost more than 60% of its value—more than $2 trillion.

CRASHES

The Tower of Terror Comes to Wall Street

A crash occurs when the total value of the stock market takes a significant nosedive. This often happens when a bubble bursts and most stockholders try desperately to sell off their shares at the same time. When more people want to sell than buy, prices drop dramatically, and investors begin to incur huge losses.

Not every big drop in total market value is considered a crash, though. Sometimes, stock prices dip because they're simply higher than they should be, and investors suddenly realize that. This kind of dip is called a correction. Corrections differ from crashes in two very important ways: They're smaller drops, and they don't last as long. As scary as corrections may seem to nervous shareholders, they really indicate a return to sensible investing.

Market crashes, on the other hand, can be terrifying. The two worst in American history are the crashes of 1929 and 1987. Other noteworthy crashes are those of 2010, 2015, and 2020.

THE CRASH OF 1929

Between the beginning of September 1929 through the end of October 1929, the stock market saw an enormous 40% drop. That decline continued until the market hit rock bottom in the summer of 1932, when it was almost 90% down from its former peak in early 1929.

But before that terrible crash, the market and its investors were flying high. After emerging victorious from World War I, Americans were full of confidence and hope, and believed the stock market would make everyone filthy rich. So, they poured all of their money into the market without asking any questions.

Some unscrupulous swindlers took advantage of their optimism, and they joined forces to influence stock prices by trading shares among themselves. They made it look like the prices were going up substantially, a practice colorfully known as "painting the tape." That enticed excited investors to buy, while the swindlers sold for artificially inflated prices and made enormous profits.

In fact, just two weeks before the bottom fell out, the Dow Jones Industrial Average index climbed to 386.10, a height that wouldn't be reached again until 1954. After that peak, the Dow declined steadily, and the pace of the fall began to quicken.

Ticker Trivia

In 1929, the Dow included companies like Chrysler, General Foods, Sears Roebuck & Company, US Steel, and General Electric.

By Wednesday, October 23, 1929, the Dow had dropped to 305.85, with 6.3 million shares trading. The next day was marked by a tide of selling. When the market opened the next Monday morning, the Dow opened low, dropped, and closed down 13%.

As the opening bell rang on Tuesday, October 29, the market was flooded with sell orders. Under that pressure, prices fell right away. In the first thirty minutes of trading, 3.3 million shares changed hands. Everyone wanted to sell, accepting whatever bids they could to close out their positions. Damaging losses were widespread, and the Dow dropped to a devastating low of 212.33. On that single day, now known as Black Tuesday, trading volume hit a record 16.4 million shares.

THE CRASH OF 1987

It was the largest single-day drop in history. On October 19, 1987, now known as Black Monday, the American stock market lost $500 billion, and the Dow suffered a 22.6% loss in a single trading session.

This sharp downturn led some conservative analysts to warn of a bubble effect. Despite the valiant efforts of the Securities and Exchange Commission (SEC), investors—even large institutional investors—weren't listening to logic. The drama of hostile takeovers and IPOs excited investors, and stock prices shot up to undreamed of levels.

By the middle of October, the economic forecast looked bleak: The dollar was down, and the United States was experiencing a large trade deficit. Investors reacted to the dreary news, and the market began to see losses on a daily basis. At the close of trading on Friday, October 16, the Dow posted a 4.6% loss, and investors got even more nervous.

By the time the US markets opened the next Monday morning, the rest of the world had seen similar declines, especially in the Asian markets. When the opening bell on the NYSE rang that day, the Dow began its descent immediately, finally sliding down 508 points.

What followed that dark day was different than the sustained economic troubles of the crash of 1929. The economy didn't plunge into a recession; there was no run on the banks. And the markets made a quick recovery, gaining back about half of their Black Monday losses in just a couple of trading sessions. In fact, it would take only two short years for the Dow to exceed its precrash high.

THE FLASH CRASH OF 2010

The flash crash of 2010 was marked by a 600-point drop in the Dow and a substantial single-day dive in the S&P 500, a 7% decline that took place in under fifteen minutes on the afternoon of May 6. That quick drop was matched by an equally speedy recovery, leaving investors and regulators puzzled. In a knee-jerk reaction, exchanges canceled more than 20,000 trades that took place during the drop, all deals completed at unusually low prices.

This flash crash was caused in part by steep declines in specific stocks, including Philip Morris, Procter & Gamble, and Accenture (which dropped all the way down to one penny per share before rebounding).

On June 10, 2010, the SEC officially enacted regulations to make sure such an alarming incident couldn't recur. These rules automatically halt trading activity for any S&P 500 stock if its share price drops (or rises) more than 10% in five minutes.

In April 2015, US authorities arrested London resident Navinder Sarao in connection with the flash crash of 2010. Sarao was charged with twenty-two crimes, including fraud, for his alleged role in the market manipulation. He pleaded guilty in November 2016.

THE FLASH CRASH OF 2015

On August 24, 2015, investors woke to a market panic as the S&P 500 plummeted almost 100 points, a 5% drop, within minutes of the opening bell. This flash crash followed a trend toward sell-offs the week before. When the Shanghai Stock Exchange Composite Index (SHCOMP) dipped more than 8% on Monday morning, US traders rushed to sell—but no one was buying, and some stocks (shares trading on the major exchanges) literally had no ready market. As more investors and traders trickled into the market, liquidity improved. Throughout the day, the S&P 500 recovered some of its loss, but it still closed down by more than 3%.

THE CRASH OF 2020

March 9, 2020, marked the beginning of the most recent stock market crash, with the Dow plummeting 2,013.76 points, a nearly 8% drop. Just a few days later, on March 12, the Dow took another huge dive, losing a record-breaking 2,352.60 points. On March 16, the Dow lost 12.93% of its value. The Dow posted its worst first quarter ever. During the same period, the S&P 500 dropped by 34%. The losses were so sharp that the NYSE had to halt trading several times during the period. The stock market was officially in crash mode.

This crash was triggered by the onset of the COVID-19 pandemic, when uncertainty flooded the world. Lockdowns, quarantines, and travel restrictions had the public in a panic. The global economy was suffering. Millions of Americans lost their jobs to shutdowns.

But largely due to government interventions like Economic Impact Payments and lowered interest rates, the stock market rebounded fairly quickly. And by the end of the year, the Dow was back up over 30,000.

PANICS

A Stampede for the Exit

When stock prices start falling fast, investors get caught up in panic selling. A panic can be focused on one company or industry, or hit the market as a whole depending on investor confidence and sentiment. During a panic, investors just want out, no matter how little money they can get for their shares. They trade on emotion rather than information. In the worse cases, panic sell-offs result in market crashes.

Most major stock exchanges have some kind of safety net in place to curb panic selling and to give investors time to absorb the fast-flying information. The hope here is that after a brief pause, the market can return to trading more normally. The NYSE, for example, has a set of "circuit breaker" rules in place to halt trading under specific circumstances.

Panic over the fall of a company's share price can spread quickly, like a virus, often infecting a whole industry. And if that virus isn't stopped, it can take down the whole market.

Two Sides of Panic

Though most panics involve selling, panic buying can occur too. This happens when investors desperately try to get in on a hot stock before its price levels off so that they don't miss out on big profits.

When a company is the initial focus of panic selling, that's usually because something has occurred that makes investors think a company's fundamental value is going to decrease. These events can include an SEC investigation, a scandal, a patent loss, or a big lawsuit. For example, when the Volkswagen emissions scandal made headline news, investors rushed to sell their shares, and the stock price took years to start to recover.

THREE BLACK DAYS

Devastating days for the financial markets are called black days. These notorious days mark catastrophic drops in market value, as benchmark indexes plunge and investors suffer enormous losses.

The first of these financial disasters came on September 24, 1869, Black Friday. It came about when a pair of infamous investors sought to corner the gold market and failed. That market collapsed, and it dragged the US stock market down with it.

The most notorious black market day occurred in 1929: Black Tuesday. On Tuesday, October 29, 1929, the US stock market tanked, setting off the Great Depression.

On another fateful October day, Black Monday, the Dow dropped by more than 20%. That took place on October 19, 1987, and it was the biggest single-day decline the market ever saw. Unlike other market catastrophes, this one wasn't brought on by a specific definable event.

THE 2008 MARKET DEBACLE

In the beginning of 2007, the titanic investment bank Bear Stearns failed after suffering huge losses when the housing bubble collapsed. Heavily involved with subprime mortgage investments, Bear

Stearns crumbled. Slowly it pulled the rest of Wall Street down with it, though that would take a little while.

By December 2007, recession hit the United States, and the Dow began its downward slide. By the summer of 2008, the benchmark index fell below 11,000.

Another blow came in September, when Lehman Brothers, another giant investment firm, declared the largest bankruptcy that had ever been filed (at the time).

The stock market responded dramatically. The day after the Lehman Brothers announcement, the ill-fated September 15, 2008, the Dow fell by 499 points.

Three days later, on September 18, the government began to talk about a bailout. That helped the Dow gain back 410 points. On the news of a potential $1 trillion TARP (Troubled Asset Relief Program) plan to help avert a complete financial meltdown and an SEC temporary halt to shorting financial company stocks, the market surged forward again. The Dow jumped up another 361 points the next day, to a close of 11,388. But that rebound proved fleeting.

After a series of devastating events, including a bank run and problems with the TARP, the Dow fell to a midday low of 7,882 on October 10, an unprecedented 3,500-point drop from its high on September 19.

THE COVID-19 PANIC OF 2020

The coronavirus calamity of 2020 had people panic shopping for diapers, toilet paper, and bottled water while simultaneously triggering a panic selling spree in the stock market. Uncertainty and fear led to negative investor sentiments and stock market uncertainty around the world. Job loss sparked financial anxiety in millions of Americans, and that contributed to a mass stock sell-off.

Investors worried about the possible effects on their health and on the health of the economy in those early COVID-19 days, before there was a vaccine or treatment, and the news was led by rapidly climbing numbers. Panic selling ensued, leading to huge daily drops in the market during March 2020, including a drastic 13% drop on March 16.

THE SVB PANIC OF 2023

Silicon Valley Bank (SVB) was among the top twenty biggest banks in the US until March 2023 when it was shut down by regulators. The bank failed after it experienced a sharp decline in the value of its investments, followed by a run on the bank where depositors began pulling out their money.

SVB was known as a business bank specializing in start-up and venture-backed companies. It stood behind a large percentage of tech and healthcare IPOs in 2022.

On March 9, SVB stock tanked when the market opened. On March 10, regulators stopped trading of SVB shares. Investors panicked, and soon other banking and financial service stocks decreased dramatically. The top ten bank stocks, which include Wells Fargo and Bank of America, were hit hard, losing a collective $76 billion in share value in a single day (March 13). Between March 8 and March 13, Bank of America stock dropped by $32 billion, and Wells Fargo by $18 billion.

THE SEC

Someone Has to Keep the Paperwork Straight

During the Great Depression, Congress passed the Securities Exchange Act of 1934 creating the US Securities and Exchange Commission (SEC). The 1934 act was designed to restore confidence in capital markets by setting clear rules and giving the SEC power to regulate the securities industry. Basically, the SEC watches over the securities industry to make sure no illegal activity takes place. To help with that enormous task, the agency sets strict standards for brokers, investors, and publicly traded corporations. Every corporation whose stock trades on a US exchange must be registered with the SEC.

The agency's main goal is to protect investors by making sure the securities markets remain honest and fair. One way the SEC meets this goal is by making sure publicly traded companies disclose enough accurate information about their business so that investors can make informed decisions. There's a never-ending slew of paperwork and disclosures required of all companies whose stocks trade on the public markets, including annual audited financial statements. In addition to keeping close tabs on publicly traded companies, the SEC also regulates any companies involved with trading and any professionals who offer investment advice.

Most important, though, the SEC is all about you: protecting you from swindles, providing you with reliable information, and keeping your broker in line.

FORMS 10-K AND 10-Q

The SEC requires that all publicly traded companies publish and file regular financial reports. The paperwork (though now it's mainly submitted electronically) provided to the SEC for annual or quarterly reports is called Form 10-K or Form 10-Q, respectively. The point of these hundred-odd-page, very dry reports is to offer investors a complete picture of the company's financial status, which is why successful investors bite the bullet and read them.

A corporation's 10-Q reports are filed for the first three quarters every year, due thirty-five days after the fiscal quarter closes. Instead of a fourth-quarter 10-Q, the corporation files its annual 10-K report. The 10-Q and 10-K reports contain a wealth of information about the company, including an overview of the business, financial statements and disclosures, and a look at corporate management (including things like executive compensation and upcoming or ongoing legal proceedings).

Form 8-K Falls in Between

Sometimes, a major issue comes up that doesn't quite fit into the standard reporting timetable. When that happens, corporations file a Form 8-K to let investors know what's going on in great detail. Events that can trigger an 8-K filing include things like selling off major assets, replacing a CEO, or plans to acquire another company.

Most investors don't want to read every word in these long reports, but it's important to hit the highlights. On the numbers front, you'll need to do a little math and analysis of your own, such as comparing this year to last, or comparing actual profits to expectations. Reading through the Management Discussion section lets investors know what's going on behind those numbers, how things are changing, and what management expects to happen going forward. Finally, the footnotes to the financial statements offer the investors their best chance of sniffing out suspicious or creative accounting practices.

ACCREDITED INVESTORS

Not all investors are the same in the eyes of the SEC. Investors with more experience and wealth, called accredited investors, don't need as much protection. Because of that, these investors can participate in high-risk (and highly lucrative) investments that are not available to the rest of us.

To qualify as an accredited investor for SEC purposes (defined in SEC Regulation D, Rule 501), an investor must:

- Earn income of at least $200,000 a year ($300,000 for a married couple) for the most recent two years, and reasonably expect that level of income to continue OR
- Have at least $1 million net worth (individual or joint with a spouse), not including the primary residence (a condition added in 2010) OR
- Be intimately involved as a partner, director, or executive officer in the company issuing the stock

Accredited investors can be people, but they're equally likely to be big companies themselves, like insurance companies or banks. No government agency actually confirms that someone really is an accredited investor; that responsibility lies with whoever is selling the security. Beginning in 2013, the SEC published stricter guidance for people and companies selling restricted investments to accredited investors in an attempt to verify that these investors really are eligible to invest.

Investments open to accredited investors that are not available to the general public include private equity, hedge funds, venture capital, and unregistered securities.

Because these securities are not subject to the same disclosure regulations as those issued by publicly traded companies, and because sellers are not required to share specific information with potential investors, these are considered to be high-risk investments.

EDGAR

EDGAR is like a convenience store for information about corporations. With a few mouse clicks, potential investors can find all the information they need about any company listed on the major exchanges within minutes. The SEC's comprehensive database, known as EDGAR (Electronic Data Gathering, Analysis, and Retrieval), was created in 1984. EDGAR holds a complete database of all corporate reports filed by public companies and complaints filed against the companies all the way back through 1994, more than 70 million pages of documents, with approximately 3,000 new documents filed every day. This gives individual investors access to the same information at the same time as massive institutional investors.

On the SEC website (www.sec.gov), you can visit this special section and quickly find the information you need to make the best investment decisions.

It's very easy to search EDGAR for information on any company you plan to invest in, making it a great first stop. You can enter either the company name or ticker symbol to begin your search. Using EDGAR, you can gain access to every document a corporation has ever filed with the SEC. Because the wealth of information can quickly become overwhelming, you would do well to focus your review on specific documents. Specific types of filings you should consider searching for include Form 10-Q, quarterly report; Form 10-K, annual report; 8-K, current report; Form 11-K, employee stock purchase and savings plans; ARS, the annual report to securities holders; and DEF 14A, proxy statements.

Using EDGAR for the first time can be confusing, so the SEC provides detailed instructions about how to get the most out of your searches. When you run a search, the documents will show up in date order, with the most recent filing appearing first. Using the simple filters at the top of the document lists, you can enter which type of filing you want to see. You can import EDGAR documents directly into Microsoft Excel, which makes it easy to perform a do-it-yourself analysis on the company's financial data.

ECONOMIC INDICATORS

What's Driving This Train?

When it comes to understanding the economy, data is king. Information about everything from how weather affects crops to changes in employment rates to oil prices helps economists and stock analysts alike figure out how they expect the markets to move. That includes the stock market, which is sensitive to many economic indicators.

Economic indicators are used by financial forecasters to predict what will happen next, and then traders base buy and sell decisions on that critical information. These indicators are comprised of collections of statistical and survey data, which is bundled into neat numerical packages and released to the public. Broad economic indicators are used to forecast sweeping market trends.

INFLATION AND DEFLATION

The state of the economy greatly influences the stock market. Whether the economy is growing, stagnating, or contracting, stock markets react. Two major economic states that affect stock prices are inflation and deflation.

Inflation

Inflation is clearly marked by rising prices and falling purchase power. Because every dollar you have is worth less than it was before, it now costs more to buy the same things. Inflation, when it remains in a manageable 2% to 3% range, is the normal state of the economy. As prices increase, wages and stock prices tend to follow suit in a healthy economy. But when inflation skyrockets such that it greatly exceeds increases in income, the markets can't compensate. When purchasing power declines too much and too fast, people don't buy as much, and companies start to feel the pinch. Corporations begin posting shrinking profits, causing stock prices to drop.

Runaway Inflation

The US economy saw disastrous inflation in the mid-1970s. While stock market returns hovered at around 6% or 7%, inflation clocked in at nearly double that, rising to more than 13% by 1979. And though it hasn't reached that height since, 2021 was marked by unusually high inflation of 7%, mainly due to the effects of COVID-19.

Deflation

Deflation is an overall decrease in prices. This sounds like it would be a good thing, but it isn't. Typically, deflation is brought on by a widespread reduction in personal or government spending, drying up demand for goods and services. This triggers tighter credit policies (making it harder to borrow money) and rampant unemployment. Deflation then causes a run of unfortunate and self-sustaining events such as plummeting corporate profits, downsizing, plant closings, shrinking salaries, loan defaults, increased bankruptcies, and decreasing stock prices. This confluence of events can set off panic selling in the stock market, bringing it to the brink of a crash. Prolonged periods of deflation can set off a recession or, even worse, a depression.

MARKET TRENDS

From terrorist attacks to changing weather patterns, from technological innovations to shifts in consumer tastes, the market reacts to a wide array of factors. Some of these factors are temporary, and some are permanent. From an investor's perspective, identifying major and permanent trends is the key to consistently profiting in the stock market.

Major short-term trends, which last for months or years, can happen in reaction to "black swan" events. For example, terrorist attacks in Europe affect international travel and tourism, which in turn affect the stock prices of companies in the travel industry.

Permanent, or fundamental, changes last forever; there's no going back. The constant flow of information on the Internet gave birth to e-commerce, instant global communication, and limitless entertainment. Video streaming services like Netflix, Hulu, and Disney+ have made cable television essentially obsolete. Spotify and YouTube transformed the way we listen to and experience music. Companies that don't see and adapt to these seismic changes are destined to disappear.

Sometimes trends come from consumers themselves, like the boom in gluten-free and dairy-free foods. Even Ben & Jerry's now offers dairy-free and gluten-free ice cream products. The dizzying array of gluten-free cookies, breads, and pastas nearly fill up as much space on the grocery shelves as the wheat-filled products they imitate.

Market trends can also be shaped by government actions, like interest rate adjustments, new tax laws, or increased spending. International trade agreements can regulate the flow of imports and exports, having a pointed impact on the stock market.

LEADING, LAGGING, AND COINCIDENT

There are three main types of indicators: leading, lagging, and coincident. Each offers a different way to assess the direction of the economy, which strongly influences the direction of the stock market.

Economic factors that change before the overall economy changes, offering some insight into what comes next, are called leading indicators. As you might expect, these indicators are not always right, but decades of experience show us that they very often offer reliable predictive information for investors. Traders and analysts make their bets based on these indicators of where the economy is headed.

Lagging indicators do just what their name implies: They follow on the heels of a change in the economy or the stock market. Analysts primarily use these indicators to confirm that a change is taking place. One of the most commonly quoted lagging indicators is the unemployment report. Here, unemployment refers to people who are not currently working but could be, calculated as the total number of unemployed people divided by the full potential labor force. When this number increases, it's a sign of existing economic struggle and it typically doesn't decrease until the economy is well into its recovery.

Coincident indicators happen right along with changes in the economy. For example, when the economy is strong, people's income increases. Like lagging indicators, coincident indicators help confirm the country's economic health.

THE GDP

Gross domestic product, or GDP, is the most widely used economic indicator as it tracks the overall wellness of the country's economy. It's a measure of all the goods and services sold within the country during a particular period of time, usually a quarter (three months). Economists and stock traders track the GDP over time to measure the economy's health. GDP growth instills confidence and optimism in investors, generally leading to increasing trade volume and share prices.

HEMLINES AND LIBRARIES

Not all economic indicators are carefully calculated and compiled in stuffy rooms lined with supercomputers. Some of the most popular—and weirdest—indicators look directly at how certain people and events affect the market.

How do hemlines affect the economy? Historically, when hemlines go up and skirts get shorter, the economy and the stock market have tended to rise as well. Longer skirts have coincided with declining stock prices. Experts believe this lagging indicator has held true because people show off more skin when times are good, and that's also when they invest more heavily in the stock market.

Then there's the library indicator, which gauges the strength of the economy based on the number of library visitors. This phenomenon, discovered by librarians rather than economists, shows that library use increases during recession. People visit more, check out more books, and use more online library services during tough economic times.

Presidential approval ratings are also rumored to affect the stock market, but not the way you'd expect. As it turns out, the Dow does better when the majority of Americans don't like the president, and approval ratings sit between 35% and 50%.

STOCK INDEXES

Big Baskets of Corporations

"The Dow closed up 120 points today." "Stocks were mixed at today's closing."

You've no doubt heard these words at the end of newscasts, in radio updates, and at cocktail parties. And while the general idea of these snippets is fairly clear, what stands behind them takes a bit of untangling.

These days in the world of finance, traders, newscasters, and stock analysts use market indexes to track investment performance, and there are literally hundreds of indexes published now.

A stock index is a collection of different stocks; sometimes they're grouped by specific characteristics (a small-cap stock index, for example), and other times they reflect the market itself. Some indexes track very broad sections of the market, while others have a more pointed focus. Using the right indexes as benchmarks will help you gauge just how well, or how poorly, particular stocks are performing—as long as you choose the right index for comparison.

When analysts and brokers are talking about market performance, they'll often refer to an index to measure prices or volume. Three of the most talked about stock indexes in the United States are the Dow Jones Industrial Average (the Dow), the S&P 500, and the NASDAQ Composite, but those are just a few of the hundreds of indexes available for comparison. Other important indexes to follow include the NASDAQ 100, the Russell 2000, and the Wilshire 5000.

THE DOW

A Basket of Influence and Stature

Formally known as the Dow Jones Industrial Average (or DJIA), the Dow is among the most widely recognized measures of American stock market performance. Virtually every report on the US stock market includes the daily movement of this iconic index, even if they don't include any other financial information.

When reporter Charles H. Dow created the index in 1896, it tracked a group of twelve industrial corporations including General Electric, the only company still listed in the index. He published that information in his "Customers' Afternoon Letter," which transformed into today's *Wall Street Journal*. The Dow expanded to include thirty companies back in 1929.

Though the Dow follows the stocks of only thirty US companies, they are among the largest and most influential corporations. All of the stocks that comprise the Dow are considered blue chips, the most prestigious, reliable corporations, and they're all actively traded on the NYSE.

Despite its familiar name, the Dow isn't really a true average anymore, and it doesn't include only what most people would consider "industrial" companies. In fact, McDonald's, Apple, Verizon, and Nike all have places in the Dow. The editors of *The Wall Street Journal* decide which thirty corporations make the list, and which get cut. Famous companies that have been dropped from the Dow include Sears, AT&T, and General Motors.

POINTS, WEIGHTS, AND THE DOW DIVISOR

When the Dow is talked about in the news, reporters refer to "points" rather than dollars: "The Dow rose by 116 points," for example. While many people just assume that points mean the same thing as dollars here, they don't. Rather, using points is a simpler way to indicate changes in the index. The points are connected to dollars, but it is not a simple one-to-one ratio, and that's largely because of the way the Dow gets calculated, by means of the Dow Divisor.

Essentially, the Dow is a price-weighted index. Its value is based on the current share price of each stock in the index. Here's where it gets different, and a little tricky: Rather than just dividing that total value by the number of stocks in the index (like you would for a true average), that total gets divided by a special divisor called the Dow Divisor.

Originally, the Dow Divisor was exactly equal to the number of different stocks in the index, and so was a calculation of a true average. But events over time required a change in the computation. To counteract the impact of occurrences like stock splits, stock dividends, and changes in the makeup of the list, the Dow Divisor was established. For example, if a stock trading for $90 per share underwent a three-for-one split (meaning a stockholder would now have three shares for every one she held before), the share price would artificially drop to $30 per share because of the split even though there would be no real change in the stock's value. The Dow Divisor adjusts for circumstances like this to make sure they don't distort the overall index value.

Because many of the companies on the list have undergone splits and the like, the Dow Divisor has shrunk substantially over time. As of November 2023, the divisor itself was equal to 0.1517. Armed with that information, we can figure out the dollar change in the Dow based on its point change. For example, if the Dow were up 300 points, that number would convert to a dollar gain of approximately $45.51 (calculated as 300 points multiplied by 0.1517).

Because the Dow is a price-weighted index, stocks with higher prices count (or weigh) more than lower-priced shares. That means a stock trading for $100 per share counts five times more than a stock trading for $20 per share. So smaller swings in higher-priced stocks can end up having a bigger impact on the Dow than a relatively huge change in a lower-priced stock.

THE DOW BY NUMBERS

To get a true sense of the historic rise and fall of the US stock market, all you need to do is look back at the Dow. Even a brief glance at some of its most memorable moments will let you see the market's most glorious highs and heartbreaking lows, and how the passage of time affects overall stock prices. In the following table, (I) indicates an intraday (or midday) quote; (C) indicates the quote at market close.

DOW VALUE	QUOTE TIME	DATE
100.25	(C)	January 12, 1906
381.70	(C)	September 3, 1929
230.00	(C)	October 29, 1929
41.22	(C)	July 8, 1932
150.94	(C)	February 4, 1936

500.24	(C)	March 12, 1956
1,003.16	(C)	November 14, 1972
2,002.25	(C)	January 8, 1987
1,738.74	(C)	October 19, 1987
10,006.78	(C)	March 29, 1999
11,722.98	(C)	January 14, 2000
7,286.27	(C)	October 9, 2002
14,198.10	(I)	October 11, 2007
6,469.95	(I)	March 6, 2009
11,205.03	(C)	April 27, 2010
15,056.20	(C)	May 7, 2013
18,312.39	(C)	May 19, 2015
27,088.08	(C)	July 11, 2019
36,952.65	(C)	January 5, 2022

With a rich history woven through its ups and downs, the Dow Jones Industrial Average reflects not just the stock market, but the changing moods, landmark events, and economic shifts in the United States and the world.

The Dow Changes Hands

Though the index still bears its iconic name, Dow Jones & Company doesn't own it anymore. In July 2012, the Dow and the S&P 500 came together to become the largest single source of market indexes in a joint venture between S&P Global and the CME Group.

S&P 500

Tracking the Roller Coaster

Though this index was launched in the 1950s, its seeds were planted nearly 100 years earlier, when Henry Poor published a groundbreaking work called *History of the Railroads and Canals of the United States*. Despite what that title suggests, this book traced the financial history of the companies involved in those two defining industries, furthering Poor's intent to spread financial information to the public. And it was so successful that Poor began to publish every year.

Inspired by that success, more companies joined the financial tracking game, including two key players: Standard Statistics and John Moody & Company. Standard Statistics soon led the pack, creating an index that at first tracked more than 200 stocks in many different market sectors. That number dropped to ninety because, back then, it was impossible to track more companies—they didn't have computers to do the work.

When Henry Poor's company went under after the big crash of 1929, it was gobbled up by Standard Statistics...and the Standard & Poor's 90 Index was born. Back then, this was the only index calculated daily.

The index was finally able to expand when it computerized in 1946. Using an IBM punch card computer, the company gained the capability to track 500 companies, and update their statistics every hour.

Officially launched in March 1957, the Standard & Poor's 500 Index was (and is still) made up of 500 leading companies. The corporations included in this index are intended to represent the broader economy. Changes in the economy can lead to changes in the makeup of the index, as companies are dropped (like Sears, Dell, and Avon) and others are added.

Out of the possible candidates, corporations are chosen for the list by a committee at Standard & Poor's, now one of the nation's leading investment companies. In order to qualify for inclusion in this prestigious list, officially called the Constituent List, companies must meet specific criteria, such as:

- At least $14.5 billion total market capitalization
- Positive earnings over the most recent consecutive four quarters
- US companies only

The S&P 500 is a market-capitalization weighted index, meaning companies with larger market capitalization count more than smaller companies. As a company's share price climbs, it adds more to the overall return of the index. Though the S&P 500 includes only a selection of stocks, many analysts and traders consider it to be a benchmark for the stock market as a whole.

Companies found in today's S&P 500 Constituent List include Apple (AAPL), Tesla (TSLA), and Amazon.com (AMZN). The most recent additions (as of September 2023) include Airbnb (ABNB) to replace Newell Brands (NWL), and Blackstone (BX) to replace Lincoln National Corp. (LNC).

Ticker Trivia

The S&P 500 Index is not connected with the *Fortune* 500, though they include many of the same companies. The main difference is that the *Fortune* 500 includes privately owned corporations, while the S&P 500 includes only publicly traded companies.

NASDAQ COMPOSITE

It's Not Just Tech Stocks Anymore

First formed on February 5, 1971, the NASDAQ Composite index includes more than 2,500 stocks, all of which are listed on the NASDAQ exchange. Unlike other stock indexes, the NASDAQ Composite includes other types of equities (like real estate investment trusts, or REITS) rather than only traditional corporate common stock, and not all of the companies included are headquartered in the United States.

Like the S&P 500, the NASDAQ Composite is a market-capitalization weighted index. Because it includes mainly technology and Internet companies, which are businesses that tend to be more volatile, this index can swing pretty widely. However, other industries are represented as well, including finance and banking, consumer products, transportation, and industrial supplies.

Ticker Trivia

The NASDAQ actually maintains several different indexes, including some that are separated by industry, such as banking, biotechnology, computer, industrial, insurance, and transportation.

This index includes companies like Apple (AAPL), Amazon.com (AMZN), Microsoft (MSFT), Alphabet (GOOGL), Costco (COST), Adobe (ADBE), and Netflix (NFLX).

NASDAQ 100

A Basket of Innovation

A subset of the NASDAQ Composite index, the NASDAQ 100 includes the largest (based on market capitalization) and most actively traded 100 corporations listed on the NASDAQ stock exchange. Launched in January 1985, the NASDAQ 100 has become one of the most tracked indexes in the world with its roster of innovative corporations. Though more than half of these companies fall under the tech umbrella (down from nearly 70% back in 2001), other industries are represented as well, like consumer staples, healthcare, and telecommunications.

Corporations found in the NASDAQ 100 (as of September 2023) include:

- Intel (INTC)
- Ross Stores (ROST)
- Starbucks (SBUX)
- Dollar Tree (DLTR)
- eBay (EBAY)
- Tesla (TSLA)
- Microsoft (MSFT)
- T-Mobile (TMUS)
- Costco (COST)
- Netflix (NFLX)
- Meta (META)

Included in this index, investors will find both US and international corporations listed on the NASDAQ. They remain in the index as long as their average daily trading volume hits at least 200,000 shares. The only companies specifically excluded from the NASDAQ 100 belong to the financial industry.

Over the past couple of decades, this index has become more "grown up," as the companies listed on it evolved. For example, over the five-year period from 2008 to 2013, the average market capitalization of corporations listed on the NASDAQ 100 grew by nearly 400%, from $435 million in 2008 to $1.6 billion in 2013. Now, nearly half of the companies included in this index pay regular shareholder dividends, underscoring their success.

RUSSELL 2000

A Look at the Little Guys

Unlike the other indexes we've discussed so far, which focus on large companies, the Russell 2000 index follows 2,000 of the smallest companies listed on the US stock exchanges. You probably haven't even heard of the overwhelming majority of them, and some of the more familiar listings may surprise you.

Ticker Trivia

The Russell 2000 is home to small-cap corporations, companies with market capitalization between $300 million and $2 billion. In contrast, large-cap companies like those counted in the S&P 500 have market capitalization of at least $10 billion.

Since these companies are less established, make less money, and hold fewer assets than the companies on the S&P 500 and the Dow, they are more vulnerable to changes in the economy. Because of this, the Russell 2000 is one of the most volatile indexes covering the US stock market.

Created in 1984 by the Frank Russell Company, this market value-weighted index was the first small-cap benchmark for investors. The Russell 2000 cuts across virtually every industry, and focuses on up-and-coming corporations rather than industry leaders. With an average market capitalization hovering at around $2.96 billion, these companies may not seem small. But in the stock market pond they swim in, they're the smallest fish around.

The Russell 2000 includes:

- e.l.f. Beauty (ELF)
- Super Micro Computer (SMCI)
- Murphy Oil (MUR)
- Simpson Manufacturing (SSD)
- Chord Energy (CHRD)
- ChampionX (CHX)
- Chart Industries (GTLS)

Stocks that trade for less than $1 per share, or that are listed on the pink sheets, are specifically excluded from the Russell 2000.

FT WILSHIRE 5000

The Whole Enchilada

Though it's not as well known, the FT Wilshire 5000 Index (FTW5000) is the largest index (by market value) in the world.

When it was first created back in 1974, the index was comprised of 5,000 stocks. Don't let the name fool you, though: The FT Wilshire 5000 now includes only 2,196 corporations, a number that changes quite often along with the number of companies listed on the major stock exchanges. That number has undergone some seismic shifts since its creation, with an all-time high of 7,562 companies in 1998, followed by a steady decline. December 2005 was the last time the index actually included at least 5,000 corporations.

Ticker Trivia

The FT Wilshire 5000 gets updated every second on the NASDAQ ticker.

This index keeps track of virtually all of the publicly traded companies that are headquartered in the United States and traded on one of the American stock exchanges, and because of that it's often called the Total Stock Market Index. To be included in the FT Wilshire 5000, a company's share price has to be readily available to the general public.

The FT Wilshire 5000 is a capitalization-weighted index, which means larger companies count more than smaller ones when the index value is calculated. If a large company's stock has a big price swing, it would affect the index value more than if a smaller company had an even bigger price swing.

MARKET CAPITALIZATION

From XS to XXXL, Size Matters

When it comes to the stock market, size matters. And, here, size is measured in terms of market capitalization, or the market value of all of the company's outstanding shares.

To calculate the market capitalization of a company, multiply the current market price of a stock by the number of outstanding shares. The number of outstanding shares refers to the number of shares that have been sold to the public.

The math is pretty straightforward: A publicly traded corporation that has 30 million shares outstanding that are currently trading for $20 each would have a market capitalization of $600 million. Although there are a few different groupings used to categorize stocks by their capitalization, these categories change over time. For example, back in the 1980s a company with a market cap of $1 billion was considered to be a large-cap corporation; in today's terms, it would fall in the small-cap category. Here's a general rule of thumb you can follow when companies are referred to in terms of their market capitalization:

- Large cap: $10 billion and over
- Mid cap: Between $2 billion and $10 billion
- Small cap: Between $300 million and $2 billion
- Micro cap: Under $300 million

The category a company falls into tells you a lot about its prospects. Large-cap companies, for example, are usually rock-solid businesses you can rely on, but don't have a lot of room for growth.

Small-cap companies, on the other hand, may be poised for explosive growth, but that potential for growth is tempered by lower market share and fewer assets, and the risk that they could easily miss the mark and disappear.

Mega and Nano

To separate out both massive and minute corporations, some analysts add in two more categories: mega cap and nano cap. Mega-cap companies have unimaginable market capitalizations that top $200 billion. On the other end of the scale are the nano caps, extremely tiny companies (at least by market standards) with a market cap under $50 million.

LARGE CAP

Large-cap (also called big-cap) stocks are the biggest players in the stock market, and tend to be the most conservative investments. Though they grab the lion's share of attention on Wall Street, these companies make up just a tiny fraction of the stock market as a whole (based on the number of companies traded). These are the companies you hear about every day.

A large-cap corporation typically has a more solidly established presence and more reliable sales and profits than smaller corporations. Most of the time, larger companies make less risky investments than smaller companies. The trade-off for this stability, though, can be slower growth rates. Many investors hold large-cap stocks for the long term, and for good reason: More than fifty years of historical market returns show that these corporate giants yield only slightly lower returns than short-term investments, and with much less volatility.

In addition, many large-cap corporations offer their shareholders a steady flow of reliable dividends. In terms of investor returns, these dividend streams help balance out the lower growth potential. Plus, it's very easy to find in-depth information about these companies, which helps investors make the best choices when they're deciding where to put their money.

Examples of large-cap stocks include ExxonMobil (XOM) with market capitalization (as of October 2023) of $418.29 billion and Walmart (WMT) with $433.80 billion. In the subcategory of mega-cap stocks, there's Apple (AAPL) with a market cap of $2.63 trillion, Microsoft (MSFT) with $2.45 trillion, and Amazon.com (AMZN) with $1.32 trillion.

MID CAP

Mid-cap stocks, as the name suggests, are bigger than small caps but smaller than large caps, and their business stage (where they fall in the continuum between start-up and maturity, typically a sustained growth phase) tends to fall right in between the two. Though these companies can offer some distinct advantages to investors, you won't hear much about them. They get much less coverage by analysts and news services than their large-cap colleagues, and so these promising companies often get overlooked. That doesn't mean, though, that they aren't worth looking into.

Companies in this grouping are often trying to increase their market share, striving to become more competitive so they can break out of the pack and become the next large-cap company. They can do this because they're successful enough to attract enough financing to expand. That growth effort gives prospective shareholders the opportunity for potentially large gains, if the company takes off.

While they may offer higher returns and more room for sustained growth than large-cap companies, mid-cap companies also come with more inherent risk (though not nearly as much as small- or micro-cap companies). From an investment standpoint, that risk is particularly important to consider. During economic downturns, these up-and-coming corporations may not have the reserves to weather business slumps.

Examples of mid-cap companies include United States Steel (X) with market capitalization of $7.49 billion (as of October 2023), Skechers USA (SKX) with $7.13 billion, Bill.com Holdings (BILL) with $9.54 billion, and Williams-Sonoma (WSM) with $9.35 billion.

SMALL CAP

The small-cap stock category includes many of the small, emerging companies that have survived their initial growing pains and are now enjoying strong earnings gains, along with expanding sales and profits. Today's small-cap stock may be tomorrow's leader—it may also be tomorrow's loser.

Small-cap corporations have much more limited resources than mid- or large-cap companies, which makes them very vulnerable to economic downturns. Often, these are very new companies, or companies in new industries, both of which come with a lot of uncertainty.

Overall, these stocks tend to be very volatile and risky, and shares undergo enormous price swings in very short periods of time. For a lucky few, though, the risk pays off when a small company makes it big.

Ticker Trivia

A safe way of adding small-cap stocks to your portfolio can be through a professionally managed fund, instead of choosing individual stocks. That way, you'll have exposure to potentially explosive profits without the high risk of loss that comes with investing in a specific small company.

MICRO CAP

According to the SEC, micro-cap stocks are defined as shares in corporations with very low market values. Their total market capitalization will be under $250 or $300 million. That sounds like a lot of money, but in the world of corporate finance it's barely a drop in the bucket.

In fact, some of these companies are so small that they aren't required to register with the SEC at all. If they have total assets under $10 million and fewer than 2,000 investors, they don't have to file anything.

Unlike larger corporations, shares in micro-cap companies trade mainly in the OTC (over-the-counter) market, on the pink sheets. And though the NASD (National Association of Securities Dealers) oversees the over-the-counter (OTC) securities market, this exchange is not part of NASDAQ. Because they're not listed on major exchanges, micro-cap stocks are not subject to listing requirements, like holding a minimum amount of assets or having a minimum number of shareholders. The latter can make it very difficult to sell your shares quickly.

Ticker Trivia

Companies with market capitalization under $50 million are sometimes referred to as nano caps.

Micro-cap stocks are very risky, and their price movement can be extremely volatile. What's more, the micro-cap market is fraught with fraud, schemers, and scams. You may find enticements in your email inbox, with headlines claiming things like "88% returns in just one day!" The prospect of amazing returns can suck in unskilled investors who are looking to make a killing. If you're planning to dive into the world of micro-cap stocks, make sure you do your homework. You need to be able to tell when you're facing a real gold mine opportunity and when there's nothing backing up the hype.

But not all micro-cap companies are scams. In fact, many of them earnestly want to become solid businesses, and grow into large caps, but that still doesn't mean they will succeed. Often saddled with a lot of debt, negative earnings, and limited assets, these hopefuls can fade away more easily than they can make a sizable splash.

MARKET SECTORS

Every Slice Has a Different Topping

Investors and analysts alike look for ways to classify stocks. This makes it easier to gauge their stocks' performance, and helps them diversify their portfolios. One of the key ways to classify stocks is by their market sector.

A market sector is a group of industries with a similar purpose. Although people use those two words—"sector" and "industry"—interchangeably, they don't mean the same thing. "Industry" refers to a group of companies that are in the same line of business. Sectors have a broader scope, capturing larger sections of the economy. Indeed, one sector may hold several industries. For example, insurance is an industry, and that industry falls in the financial sector, along with banks and brokerage firms.

Ticker Trivia

In 1900, the railroad sector was by far the biggest, making up almost 63% of the total market. The biggest sector in 2000 did not exist back then: information technology, which comprised about 23% of the 2000 market.

Sectors can be defined in many different ways, but when people refer to market sectors, they're generally referring to these eleven well-defined market segments:

1. Basic materials
2. Capital goods
3. Communications

4. Consumer cyclical
5. Consumer staples
6. Energy
7. Financial
8. Healthcare
9. Technology
10. Transportation
11. Utilities

As you might expect, different sectors flourish whiles others languish in the same economic circumstances. For example, when the economy slows down, the technology sector may decline as the utilities sector gains ground.

OWNERSHIP STATUS

This Is My Company

It's time to take an inside look at stocks, from what they are to the types available to what they can mean for your portfolio. Buy-and-hold investors invest in companies that have stood the test of time. Traders take an active approach to investing, placing more emphasis on stock price movement than on the real value of the company. Regardless of which strategy you use, you should know what and why you're buying (or selling) before you make any trade.

STOCKS ARE PIECES OF A COMPANY

Purchasing shares of stock is like buying a business. That's the way Warren Buffett, one of the world's most successful investors, views it—and his philosophy is certainly worth noting. When you buy stock, you're buying a portion of a corporation. If you wouldn't want to own the entire company, you should think twice before you consider buying even a piece of it. If you think of investing this way, you'll be a lot more cautious when reviewing a specific company.

It's important to become acquainted with all of the details of the company you're considering. What products or services does the company offer? Which parts of the business account for the greatest and least revenue? Is the company too diversified? Who are its competitors? Is there a demand for the company's offerings? Is the company an industry leader? Are any mergers and acquisitions in the works? Until you understand exactly what the company does and how well it does it, you should postpone your investment decision.

Let's say you want to buy a convenience store in your hometown. You've reviewed such factors as inventory, the quality of the company's employees, and customer service programs. In addition to selling staple grocery items, the company also sells lottery tickets and operates a gas pump. The grocery side of the business may only account for a small percentage of the overall revenue. It would be in your best interest to value each part of the business separately in order to get a complete and accurate picture of the company's profit potential. Many companies have traditionally been associated with a specific business, yet may have expanded into totally new ventures. You need to know what businesses a given company operates.

Cigarettes and Wine

The Altria Group, formerly known as Philip Morris, is primarily associated with tobacco products. But the company also profits from its popular wine subsidiary, Ste. Michelle Wine Estates. In addition, the company holds Philip Morris Capital Corporation, which is involved with the financing and leasing of major assets.

Disney, for example, has historically been associated with the Disneyland and Walt Disney World theme parks. The reality is that Disney is also involved in a host of other ventures. Among other things, this multifaceted company has interests in television, movie production (including the Marvel Cinematic Universe), and streaming service Disney+. Disney also has ABC Inc.; this division includes the ABC television network, as well as FX.

It should be increasingly clear that making money through investing requires work. The more research and thought you put into your strategy, the more likely you are to reap rewards. Although there are no guarantees in the world of investing, the odds will be more in your favor if you make educated and well-informed investment decisions. When you make an investment, you are putting your money into a public company, which allows you—as part of the public—to become an owner or to have equity in the company. That's why stocks are often referred to as equities.

WHO'S REALLY IN CHARGE?

From the board of directors to the CEO, corporate management involves a lot of decision-makers, and it can be hard to figure out who stockholders should pay attention to on any given day. Because of the way corporations are set up, there's a distance between the people who own the company and the people who run it. To make sure the people running the company act in the owners' (the stockholders) best interests, most publicly held corporations in the United States maintain a two-layer system.

Directly chosen by the shareholders, the board of directors acts as their advocate, monitoring the corporation's operations and management. The head of this group (elected by the group) is the chairman of the board, and it's his job to make sure the board operates effectively. Other board members come from both inside and outside of the company. Inside board members work for the corporation, often holding key posts in upper-level management. Outside board members don't work for the company, and their role is to offer independent and unbiased points of view.

The board's responsibilities include duties such as:

- Communicating directly with corporate executives
- Framing and tracking high-level corporate strategies

- Making sure the corporation and its management operate with integrity
- Approving the overall corporate budget
- Hiring the corporation's upper management team

That management team is responsible for implementing the strategies dictated by the board, and it is their responsibility to run the company for maximum profitability. Key players of a management team include the CEO (chief executive officer), CFO (chief financial officer), and COO (chief operations officer).

The CEO is the main person in charge of everything, and reports directly to the board. In most corporations, the CEO also sits on the board. The CFO is in charge of corporate finances and reporting. He or she prepares budgets and financial statements as required, and is responsible for the financial health of the company. The COO is the most hands-on job of the three, responsible for the operations of the company, including personnel, marketing, and sales. The CFO and the COO both report to the CEO.

THE CEO PAY SCALE

CEOs can get paid almost unimaginable amounts of money, thanks to lucrative multiyear contracts that companies use to lure them into the job. Though it seems crazy, CEO compensation is based on how they're expected to perform, rather than on how well they actually do their jobs. This seemingly bizarre norm exists because corporations want to attract the best candidates to fill their top management spots.

Tracking their true pay can be tricky, though, because it doesn't all come in the form of straight salary. Corporate executives often enjoy substantial perks, like company cars, corporate jets, and generous expense accounts in addition to their sizable salaries.

Many CEOs start with base salaries topping $1 million. That pay is guaranteed regardless of the corporation's success or failure. With higher base salaries, the CEO may be less driven to work hard to improve the company's profitability and future prospects.

Next come bonuses, but these may not work the way shareholders expect. Guaranteed bonuses are really just ways of paying a higher salary without calling it that. Performance-based bonuses require the CEO to meet specific goals, and those bonuses are only paid out when the goals are achieved. As you'd expect, CEOs who get paid more if they perform well tend to work harder at maximizing shareholder value. Setting performance goals at that level, though, is not as simple as it appears. Though it might seem obvious to tie performance to revenues, profits, or share price, external forces can greatly affect any of those measures. A CEO might make tough choices that reduce profitability one year in order to set the stage for future growth, for example, or a competitor's misfortune could trigger a sales explosion that the CEO had no hand in.

One idea that's proven most effective is to connect CEO bonuses with shares of stock (rather than stock options, securities that allow their holder to buy shares of stock at a preset guaranteed price, which can encourage the executives to artificially influence stock prices for personal gain). This links what's best for the shareholders directly to the CEO's personal wealth.

A LOOK AT THE UNREAL NUMBERS

When you get a first glimpse at a CEO's salary, you may think your eyes are playing tricks on you. They're not. Top corporate executive pay continues to grow, and the chasm between their pay and the pay of the average American is truly mind-boggling.

Consider this: According to a 2023 report by the Economic Policy Institute (a nonprofit think tank), the typical salary of a CEO working for a corporation listed on the S&P 500 was 344 times higher than the average worker. The AFL-CIO "Executive Paywatch" study revealed that the average CEO compensation package for 2022 rang in at $16.7 million a year. That's the average CEO pay, and it pales in comparison to what the highest-paid executives earn. Some of the top CEO salaries for 2022 (according to the AFL-CIO) went to:

- $253.1 million: CEO Stephen Schwarzman, Blackstone
- $226.0 million: CEO Sundar Pichai, Alphabet
- $182.1 million: CEO Stephen Scherr, Hertz Global Holdings
- $168.1 million: CEO Barry McCarthy, Peloton Interactive

Now consider this: Stephen Schwarzman's annual pay was 1,068 times higher than the median $237,000 employee salary at Blackstone according to S&P Global Market Intelligence. Since 2018, an SEC disclosure rule has required corporations to publish the CEO pay ratio, comparing the top executive's compensation to that of the median company employee.

BAD CEOS

Many, if not most, CEOs act in the best interests of the corporations they work for. Sometimes, though, the CEO is so spectacularly greedy, selfish, or incompetent that he demolishes the company, leaving stunned stockholders with intolerable losses and substantially devalued shares.

Excessive pay is just one of the ways CEOs can loot their employers. People in this position can make more than $100,000 a day, even if they're doing a terrible job. Meanwhile, they also benefit from a combination of bonuses (which are not even necessarily based on performance) and perks, like luxury cars and trips on the corporate jet.

As if that's not enough, some CEOs take even further advantage of their positions, with no regard for the shareholders they're supposed to serve. For example, they can guarantee loans for themselves, or have the corporation buy assets from other companies they own or are associated with (like a brother-in-law's office furniture company). While these types of actions are clear conflicts of interest and technically illegal, they're rarely prosecuted because it's nearly impossible to prove the legal case. After all, that brother-in-law's office furniture could truly be the best deal in town.

Take the case of former Disney CEO Michael Eisner, whose tenure was marked by drama and upheaval. To make sure every decision went his way, Eisner (as chairman) stacked the board of directors with his own picks, and that group backed some very poor choices. In 2002, the Disney stock price fell to its lowest level in eight years. By 2004, the corporation's earnings didn't even come close to Wall Street projections, disappointing analysts and shareholders alike. And during that fateful time, Eisner managed to alienate Pixar

Animation Studios, one of Disney's major holdings and most successful film partners. But none of that stopped Eisner from accepting an outrageous bonus of $7.25 million. Then, in March 2004, faced with a laundry list of failures, Eisner lost the confidence of the board, and was removed from his position as chairman of the board. Shortly after that, in March 2005, Eisner finally resigned, leaving Disney in the hands of CEO Robert Iger.

SHAREHOLDERS TAKE A STAND

When a shareholder has a vested interest in a corporation's success but doesn't approve of the way the top brass is running the company, he can take action. In fact, shareholder activism can sometimes be very successful.

To really turn the tide and make an impact, a given shareholder needs a healthy stake of the company, usually around 10%. If that active shareholder happens to have a following or a lot of influence, other shareholders will join his crusade, and that's when things really start to heat up.

With enough support, a shareholder activist can sway the vote when it comes to electing board members. New and like-minded board members can put a lot of pressure on the top executives, strongly encouraging (if not outright forcing) them to clean up their acts.

Many of the changes shareholder activists favor involve frivolous, wasteful spending by upper management. Examples of excessive spending include things like a collection of corporate jets, first-class travel accommodations, entertainment expenses, extravagant parties, and hefty bonuses unrelated to performance.

After all, the shareholders own the company; it's their money that's being spent. Many invest for the long haul, and expect the corporate management to focus on long-term growth and gains rather than on season tickets and expensive "retreats" in Las Vegas. By actively asserting their collective force, shareholders can spark the kind of change that turns lackluster performance into solid profits.

One of the most famous active shareholders is Carl Icahn. Corporate executives break into a cold sweat when he sets his sights on them. Take his involvement in Time Warner, for example. After their ill-fated merger with AOL, the company's actions sent stock prices plummeting. In 2006, dismayed by the results of the clearly failing business combination, Icahn gathered up shareholder support and demanded that some changes be made and actions be taken. Among those demands: implement cost-cutting measures to increase profitability; make a $20 billion stock buyback by the corporation; and split the troubled mega-corporation into four separate companies. The activist group won two out of three, the buyback and the expense reductions (worth $1 billion). The group also put new members on the board of directors.

SOMETIMES CORPORATIONS FAIL

Investing in the stock market has ups and downs; share prices rise and fall. Sometimes, though, it's more than market sentiment that causes an investment to tank. Not every company is successful. And, as we learned the hard way back in 2008, even very big, reputable, and seemingly stable companies can crumble into nothing.

When a public company goes bankrupt, shareholders are inevitably hurt. The stock itself is worthless on the market, so the only way investors can recoup any money at all is if there's anything left over after all the creditors are paid. Whether shareholders get any money out of the liquidation (asset sell-off) depends on several factors, including what type of stock they own.

When a public corporation goes bankrupt, it follows the same basic steps as any other company. First, the firm must sell all of its assets. With those proceeds, the company then pays off any and all debts, starting with money owed to the US government (usually back taxes, interest, and penalties). Once creditors have been satisfied, the company must pay its bondholders; not all corporations issue bonds, so some skip this step. Next on the list are preferred stockholders, with common stockholders bringing up the rear.

Much of the time, common stockholders end up with nothing. However, if there is any money left after all other claims have been paid, the common stockholders will split the pot based on the percentage of shares they hold. For example, if the company has $150,000 left, a 1% shareholder would receive $1,500.

COMMON STOCK

The Powers of Ownership

Common stocks are basic equity securities that are sold to the public, and each share constitutes ownership in a corporation. When people talk about trading shares, they're talking about common stock.

Corporations come in all sizes. You can invest in a wildly successful mega-cap company or a micro-cap company that is just beginning to show signs of growth potential. Some people prefer to buy the common stock of well-established companies, while other investors would rather invest in smaller, growth-oriented companies.

No matter what type of company fits in with your overall investing strategy, it's important to research every stock you consider buying. Just because a company has been around for decades doesn't mean it's the best investment choice for you. On top of that, companies are always changing, and it's important to make sure that the information you're reviewing is the most current available.

One of the first things to review is a company's market capitalization, or the market value of all of the company's outstanding shares. To calculate the market capitalization, multiply the current market price of a stock by the number of outstanding shares. The number of outstanding shares refers to the number of shares that have been sold to the public.

In addition to market cap, there are also different categories of stocks, enough to round out any portfolio. The variety includes blue chip, growth, cyclical, defensive, value, income, and speculative stocks.

- Blue chips are prestigious, well-known companies.
- Growth stocks are companies poised to expand their sales and markets.
- Cyclicals are strongly tied to economic ups and downs.
- Defensive stocks protect your portfolio against market downturns.
- Value stocks offer more worth than their prices imply.
- Income stocks pay steady dividends.
- Speculative stocks have the potential to skyrocket or crash.

PREFERRED STOCK

First in Line for Everything

As the name suggests, preferred stockholders who own part of a company receive preferential treatment in two very important ways: They have first dibs on dividends, and they are at the head of the line for going-out-of-business payouts, should the corporation face bankruptcy and liquidation.

Preferred stocks are hybrid securities that have almost as much in common with bonds as they do with common stock. Essentially, this type of stock comes with a redemption date and a promised dividend that gets paid regardless of the company's earnings. Also like bonds, some preferred stock can be callable, which means that the corporation has the right to buy back those shares at any time, usually for a premium over their market value. If the corporation has financial difficulties, holders of preferred stock have "seniority" and priority when it comes to dividend payments, and usually rate higher dividends than common shares.

How to Buy Preferred Stock

For investors, buying (or selling) preferred stock works the same way as trading common stock. All it takes is a call to a broker or logging into your online brokerage account to add these hybrid securities to a portfolio.

There are some drawbacks to owning preferred stock, though. As the owner of preferred stock, you normally don't have the rights that come with common stock ownership, like voting. In addition, when a company's common stock price experiences strong growth, preferred prices tend to hold steady. Finally, when a corporation has a phenomenal year and pays out giant dividends on its common shares, preferred share dividend payments are usually locked in, and those shareholders don't get to share in the company's windfall.

For income-oriented investors, however, preferred stock can make a good portfolio addition. And though they aren't as prevalent as common stock, many corporations offer preferred shares. These companies include Allstate, Wells Fargo, Capital One, and T-Mobile.

PREFERRED DIVIDENDS

When it comes to receiving dividends, preferred shareholders have priority—they get paid first. Normally, this kind of stock comes with a fixed dividend, paid out every quarter. The dividend payout is calculated based on the par value (the assigned face value of a stock share when it's originally issued) of the stock, which never changes, so shareholders always know exactly how much they're getting.

For example, if ABC Corporation issues 5 million shares of 5% preferred stock with a par value of $30 per share, every quarter they would pay out a total of $1,875,000 in dividends (5% × $30 per share × 5,000,000 shares = $7,500,000 [per year] ÷ four = $1,875,000 per quarter).

PARTICIPATING PREFERRED STOCK

In times of prosperity, common shareholders can enjoy a fatter slice of the corporate earnings in the form of bigger dividend checks, while standard preferred stockholders receive their standard percentage. This drawback to preferred shares can be overcome with a special form of the security known as participating preferred.

Participating preferred shareholders get two slices of the pie: First, they get their standard fixed percent of par dividend as promised, plus they may get a second dividend payout that is based on current corporate earnings. Typically, this double dip only comes around if the common shareholders enjoy an extraordinarily high dividend, specifically a dividend that's higher than the one the preferred shareholders are slated to get.

For example, let's say ABC Corporation offers participating preferred stock with a fixed dividend of $1.50 per share, and a second dividend payment that's activated any time the common stock dividend exceeds that. After a banner quarter, the ABC Corp. board of directors declares a $2.00 per share common stock dividend. The participating preferred shareholders would receive a total of $2.00 per share in dividends: their original $1.50 dividend plus a participation dividend of fifty cents per share.

CUMULATIVE PREFERRED STOCK

Sometimes, corporations simply don't have enough cash on hand to pay out dividends, even to preferred shareholders whose dividend payments are supposed to be guaranteed. This can happen when times are tough, and a company is barely treading water and needs every penny to keep itself afloat.

In these down times, when a corporation must suspend dividend payments in order to pay their bills (and their employees), preferred stockholders are left in the lurch. Unless, that is, they have cumulative preferred shares. Cumulative preferred shares come with what's basically a "catch-up" provision. When the company once again has ample cash on hand, these preferred shareholders are entitled to receive all of the previously skipped dividends before the common stockholders can get any dividends at all.

STOCK CLASSES

My Stock's Better Than Your Stock

Not all shares of stock are created equal. Aside from the fundamental difference between common and preferred stocks, corporations can issue customized classes of stock with special features in pretty much any way they want. The main reason a corporation would do this is to concentrate power in a particular group of shareholders, which is why the most common class distinction has to do with voting rights.

Common shares issued with extra voting rights are known as super voting shares, and their purpose is to keep corporate insiders, such as the founders and key management personnel, in charge. Most often, super voting shares come with ten votes per share, as opposed to the standard one-vote-one-share power of regular common stock. However, there's no rule limiting the number of allowable votes per share, so corporations can set them much higher than ten to one.

Super shares are usually designated as Class A, with regular shares labeled Class B. That's the standard, but not all corporations follow that convention. You would be wise to double-check if a prospective company offers stock in multiple classes. For example, when it first incorporated, Alphabet (back when it was known as Google) issued Class B shares that carried ten votes apiece for its founders and chief executives. It also issued Class A shares for the general investing public, who get one vote per share. Both classes of shares can be listed and traded on the major exchanges.

While they do have more voting power, super shares usually don't own a bigger portion of the company or its earnings than standard shares do; these facets of stock ownership remain in one-to-one proportion as regular shares.

Getting More Common

Back in 2005, about 1% of initial public offerings (IPOs) included more than one class of common stock. That number leaped up to 12% in 2014, hit 15.5% in 2015, and was at more than 20% in 2022.

Examples of companies that use a dual-class stock structure include Ford Motor Company and Meta.

A CLASSIC CLASS EXAMPLE

One of the most famous cases of a corporation with different stock classes is Berkshire Hathaway (BRK), Warren Buffett's flagship company. Berkshire Hathaway has two classes of shares, Class A and Class B, and they're as different as night and ping-pong balls.

The first glaring difference between the two share classes is price: Class A (traded as BRK.A) is priced at $503,375 per share (as of October 2023), the most expensive stock in the world; Class B (traded as BRK.B) trades at $331.71. The price of the Class A shares remains exorbitantly high because Buffett has vowed to never split the stock. He does this to attract "like-minded" investors who plan to buy the stock and hold on to it, and thus garner long-term appreciation and profits. Class A shares also come with 200-times-stronger voting rights, and the shares can be converted into Class B shares at the whim of the investor.

Class B was created back in 1996 to offer more flexibility to Berkshire Hathaway's shareholders and to allow smaller investors a chance to participate in the corporation's celebrated success. The initial 517,000 shares were launched at a price of $1,180 per share, one-thirtieth of the price of a single Class A share, at that time hovering around $34,000. In 2010, the Class B shares underwent a fifty-to-one stock split, bringing the price down from $3,476 per share to around $70 per share, keeping the stock affordable for small investors.

Ticker Trivia

Berkshire Hathaway Class B shares, also known as Baby Bs, provide a special tax benefit for Berkshire Hathaway investors: These shares can be given as gifts to heirs without triggering any gift tax as Class A shares would.

BLUE CHIPS

Silver Spoon Stocks

Of the thousands of stocks traded every day, only a few hundred are considered valuable enough to be called blue chips. Blue chips are considered to be the most prestigious, well-established companies that are publicly traded. Many of them have practically become household names. Included in this mostly large-cap mix are IBM (IBM), McDonald's (MCD), Nike (NKE), and Coca-Cola (KO). A good number of blue chip companies have been in existence for decades and still lead the pack in their respective industries. Since most of these corporations have solid track records, they are good investment vehicles for individuals who lean to the conservative side in their stock picks.

Literally Blue Chips

Back in the early 1920s, Dow Jones employee Oliver Gingold coined the phrase "blue chips" when talking about high-value corporations. He named them after the blue chips used in poker games, the highest-value chips on the table.

Let's take a look at how a portfolio can benefit from holding a blue chip stock. If you had purchased 100 shares of Walmart stock on January 31, 1990, you would have paid around $4,200. Within the next five years, Walmart called for two two-for-one stock splits, meaning you would now hold 400 shares. By January 31, 1995, your shares would have been worth $18,400—more than quadrupling your original investment. And by January 31, 2008, after yet another two-for-one split which brought your holdings up to 800 shares, your investment would have been worth $40,000, almost ten times more than your original purchase price. Walmart shares split again in 1999 (for the last time as of 2023), bringing your total shares to 1,600. By October 27, 2023, your investment would have been worth $257,872, and that doesn't even include dividends received over the years!

Most blue chip companies have market capitalization in the billions, but that's not the only criteria for inclusion into this exclusive group. What other factors land corporations in this subjective category? A solid track record of weathering economic turbulence, a creditworthy reputation, healthy financial fitness, reliable earnings, consistent growth, and steady dividends.

VALUE, INCOME, AND GROWTH STOCKS

The Stock Trifecta

Stock investing comes with three main strategies: value, income, and growth. Each has a place in your portfolio, but the proportions will differ based on your personal risk tolerance, financial goals, and timeline. Value investing focuses on scooping up bargains, buying companies whose stock price doesn't reflect their true worth. Income investing prioritizes dividend-paying stocks to produce steady cash flows. Growth investing is all about potential, picking companies expected to grow faster than the overall economy.

VALUE STOCKS

Value stocks appear inexpensive when compared to their corporate earnings, dividends, sales, or other fundamental factors. Basically, you're getting more than what you pay for, which makes it a good value. That's highly dependent on current stock prices, so a good value today might not be a good value next month. A good rule of thumb is to look for solid companies that are trading at no more than three times their book value per share. Book value is the corporation's accounting equity, which is the amount of money that would be left over if the company liquidated everything and paid off all its debts. An example of good value (at least as of September 2023) is AT&T, with a price-to-book value ratio of 1.06.

Value investors analyze companies by using such data as sales volume, earnings, and cash flow. The idea here is that value companies are truly undervalued, so their stock price doesn't truly represent how much they're worth. The value to these investors is in the potential returns that come with buying and holding a good business.

Often, value stocks are found in established industries that are no longer in vogue but have proven track records coupled with low growth expectations. Low growth just means growth rates that are lower than companies in emerging or popular industries. In times of economic uncertainty, though, value stocks may hold their own while other types of stocks falter. You can identify value stocks by their relatively low price-oriented ratios, which include price-to-book value ratio, price-to-earnings ratio (P/E ratio), price-to-sales ratio, and price-to-earnings growth ratio (PEG ratio).

Keep in mind that value stocks don't always stay in that category. If they catch investors' eyes, their prices can skyrocket and that would boot them out of value status.

INCOME STOCKS

Income stocks do just what their name suggests: provide steady passive income streams for investors. These shares come with regular dividends, sometimes big enough that people can even live off the payments alone.

Income stocks will fit the bill when generating passive income is your primary goal. Look for companies with a long history of growing dividends. One good source for finding these diamonds: the S&P 500 Dividend Aristocrats Index, which includes companies that have increased dividends for at least twenty-five years in a row. Among them are even corporations that have passed the fifty-year mark for consistent dividend growth.

Preferred stocks can also make excellent income vehicles, typically providing steady dividends and high yields. As with other types of stock, you'll want to look for a solid company with a good track record, especially when you're counting on a strong reliable income stream.

Stock Dividends

Dividend investors are often looking for steady cash payouts, but some companies issue stock dividends instead. These dividends are distributed in the form of more shares in the company, which increases your total investment. Plus, since the dividends aren't cash, they aren't subject to current income taxes (unless you sell them).

GROWTH STOCKS

Growth stocks include companies with extra strong growth potential. Many companies in this category have sales, earnings, and market share that are growing faster than the overall economy. Such stocks usually represent companies focused on research and development. Pioneers in new technologies are often growth-stock companies. Earnings in these companies are usually put right back into the business, rather than paid out to shareholders as dividends.

Growth investors want to own a piece of the fastest-growing companies around, even if it means paying a hefty price for this privilege. These companies may have outstanding management teams, highly rated developments, technological innovations, or plans for aggressive expansion into foreign markets. Growth-company stocks rarely pay significant dividends, and growth investors don't expect them to. Instead, growth companies plow their earnings right back into the business to promote even more growth. Among other things, growth investors pay close attention to company earnings. If growth investing fits in with your overall strategy, look for companies that have demonstrated strong growth over the past several years and a clear plan going forward.

A word of caution: Beware of stocks whose price seems to be growing faster than would make sense. Sometimes momentum traders will help run growth-stock prices to skyscraping levels, then sell them off, causing the stock price to plummet.

CYCLICAL STOCKS

Lather, Rinse, Repeat

Companies with earnings that are strongly tied to the economic cycle are considered to be cyclical. Economic cycles can last for months or years, but they always follow the same pattern, and they are greatly affected by the economy as a whole. When the economy picks up momentum, cyclical stocks follow this positive trend. When the economy slows down, these stocks slow down too.

Cyclical industries include car manufacturers, hotels, and airlines—things that could be considered luxuries rather than necessities. When the economy is flying high, people buy more cars and take more vacations, and these cyclical industries benefit, and cyclical stock prices rise. But when the economy slows down, and people tighten their belts, these cyclical industries typically see a huge drop in sales and earnings, and so cyclical stock prices drop.

Making money with cyclical stocks can be very tricky, and is wholly dependent on getting in and out at just the right time. To do that, you must be well versed in the ups and downs of business cycles and in tune with the economy, or you could end up losing your shirt.

Cyclical stocks would include companies like General Motors (GM), Delta (DAL), and Disney (DIS).

DEFENSIVE STOCKS

These Linebackers Protect Your Portfolio

Defensive stocks offer stable earnings and steady dividends under most economic conditions, no matter what is going on in the rest of the market. During down or uncertain times, defensive stocks are the ones to own. They are considered noncyclical, meaning they don't follow the standard economic cycles like other stocks can. For that reason, they often perform better than other stocks during down cycles. However, even when the rest of the stock market is climbing high, these solid shares tend to keep that same steady pace.

That's mainly because these companies sell products we all need all the time, and can't live without. Stocks that fall into this category include food companies, clothing companies, and utility companies. These businesses cover the basic necessities of life: food, clothing, and shelter.

Not every business that falls into one of those categories, though, would be considered defensive. Companies like General Mills, and other brands you can find in the grocery store, count as defensive stocks in the food category. Restaurant stocks, on the other hand, typically don't.

Companies considered to be defensive stocks in their respective categories can change, though that seems counterintuitive. Consider utilities: You can't run your house without electricity, heat, or water. In the past, that would have included landlines (home phones), but relatively few people still have those. This means that the old-style telephone companies are no longer defensive stocks in the utilities category, though they were for a long time. Similarly, as streaming services dominated entertainment, cable companies fell out of the defensive stock category as well.

Ticker Trivia

Don't confuse defensive stocks with defense stocks. Defense stocks refer specifically to companies that manufacture and supply items such as guns, ammunition, tanks, submarines, and missiles.

The list of defensive stocks includes titans such as General Mills (GIS), Johnson & Johnson (JNJ), and Walmart (WMT).

TECH STOCKS

Tomorrow's Trends or Yesterday's News

Technology companies cover a very broad range, from physical products like computers, semiconductors (chips), and smartphones to video game software, online retailers, and biotech (a marriage of biology and technology). They provide products and services to individuals and businesses, and constantly improve, upgrade, and create things that were once considered science fiction. Any of these types of businesses that are publicly traded count as tech stocks.

Some of the most well-known and largest technology companies include:

- Amazon.com (AMZN)
- Microsoft (MSFT)
- Netflix (NFLX)
- Apple (AAPL)
- Alphabet (GOOG)
- Meta (META)

Tech stocks typically trade for more than the corporations are worth on paper, with a lot of value placed on their expected future innovations and success. With limited cash and capital assets standard for the category, these companies trade on ideas and development. Sometimes that pays off; other times they miss the mark and the companies just disappear.

INTERNATIONAL STOCKS

Money Makes the World Go Round

Investors tend to have home country bias, keeping their investment dollars where they live. That strategy can close off avenues of greater growth and earnings potential. Plus, taking a global view of investing adds another layer of diversification to your portfolio, spreading out risk among different countries and foreign markets. It can help keep your portfolio going steady when your local market's stuck in a downward trend.

Incorporating both US and international securities in your portfolio gives you the opportunity to capture the ever-growing and changing global marketplace. Financial advisors recommend allocating anywhere from 15% to 40% of your holdings in international securities, depending on your unique situation and risk tolerance.

THREE DISTINCT INTERNATIONAL MARKETS

Before you start investing in international securities, you'll want to have a good understanding of the three main types of markets. Each comes with its own risks, liquidity issues, and political stability.

1. **Developed markets:** economically advanced nations with well-established financial markets. These are found in stable countries and have higher market capitalization, fewer liquidity issues, and more market regulations. Examples include Canada, Great Britain, and Japan.

2. **Emerging markets:** nations currently undergoing rapid industrialization and economic growth, as well as increasing household income. These are found in countries with less political and cultural stability and have lower market capitalization, less liquidity, and are just beginning to develop or refine market regulations. Examples include China, Brazil, and India.
3. **Frontier markets:** nations poised to become future emerging markets, but that aren't quite there yet. These nations are generally less developed industrially and economically, have minimal market liquidity, and the markets tend to be unregulated and much riskier for investors. Examples include Egypt, Morocco, and Senegal.

It's important to note that these definitions are loose guidelines and criteria may vary by institution. For example, one entity may classify a country in the frontier category while another includes it as emerging. That doesn't change the economic, political, or stability data about the country, just its classification by a particular institution.

DIFFERENT WAYS TO BUY FOREIGN STOCKS

When you're investing in US stocks, you basically pick a brokerage and place your order. Buying shares of non-US-based companies works differently, even when those shares are sold on US exchanges. Generally, you'll see higher fees and costs when investing internationally than you would trading US shares.

Here are four ways you can add international stocks into your portfolio:

1. **Global mutual funds and exchange-traded funds (ETFs)** are the easiest ways to get some foreign exposure. In addition to the convenience, you also get the benefits of broad diversification with a single investment. These funds may hold shares from all around the world, single market tiers (like an emerging markets fund), or single countries. Some focus on geographical areas, like Latin America, while others focus on market capitalization. You'll find both index funds and managed funds under the global heading.
2. **American Depositary Receipts (ADRs)** allow foreign shares to trade on US exchanges. They're certificates provided by American banks that represent one or more underlying shares in a foreign company; a single ADR could mean ten shares, for example, depending on the particular company. Some ADRs trade only on the OTC market, while others can trade on mainstream exchanges like the NYSE. Examples of companies that trade using ADRs include Alibaba (BABA) and Nestlé (NSRGY).
3. **Global Depositary Receipts (GDRs)** are similar to ADRs: shares trading outside their home country markets, other than the US. A bank issues the GDR to represent underlying shares of a corporation. GDRs trade on foreign exchanges, such as the London Stock Exchange, the same way stocks would, and are often quoted in US dollars.
4. **Direct investing** involves buying stock on foreign exchanges either with a US broker that offers international trading or with a local (to the exchange) brokerage account. US brokers that provide this service include Charles Schwab, Fidelity, and TD Ameritrade. Many countries support trading platforms that welcome US investors. The most popular online international brokerages include Interactive Brokers and Saxo Bank. Direct

investing is recommended for sophisticated, active investors with a strong understanding of local market and tax laws.

No matter how you choose to include foreign securities in your portfolio, it's important to do your homework. Foreign markets don't operate the same way as the US stock market and may not have the same level of regulatory security. So, before you invest any money overseas, make sure you understand all the potential risks.

INTERNATIONAL INVESTING RISKS

Just like any investment, foreign stocks come with risks. Along with the standard issues related to the market and the individual companies, though, international shares add another layer of risk. As you look into international investing, make sure to consider these potential risks: political instability, foreign exchange rate changes, currency fluctuations, limited information, regulatory issues, and higher trading costs.

When you're prepared for these risks and have a plan in place to manage their impact on your portfolio, you'll be better able to take advantage of the many benefits of international investing.

The Tax Effect

When you hold foreign stocks that pay dividends, you'll almost always be subject to foreign taxation. The tax rates vary widely based on the home country of the investment and your home country, the type of investment, and any tax treaties that apply. US citizens may be able to take a foreign tax credit on their tax returns to offset taxes paid to other countries.

PENNY STOCKS

You Get What You Pay For

Penny stocks are stocks that sell for $5 or less, and in many cases you're lucky if they're worth even that much. Most penny stocks usually have no substantial income or revenue. You have a high potential for loss with penny stocks. If you have a strong urge to invest in this type of company, take time out to follow the stock to see if it has made any headway. Learn all you can about the company, and don't be tempted to act on a hot tip that may have been passed your way.

The companies behind these stocks are thinly capitalized and are often not required to file reports with the SEC. They trade over the counter, and there is a limited amount of public information available. This in itself is reason for concern. How many astute investors want to put their money into an investment offering little or no information? Nonetheless, people do invest in these stocks.

One of the most interesting—and alarming—aspects of penny stock dealing is that brokers are not always acting as a third party but instead set prices and act as the principals in the transaction. Penny stocks most often do not have a single price but a number of different prices at which they can be purchased or sold.

Okay, so there's little information about the company, the price, or anything else to investigate. But the guy on the phone—making a cold call—says it will be the next Starbucks! This is where they get you. Thanks to the Internet and the selling of phone lists, penny stocks dealers can reach out far and wide. They use high-pressure sales tactics and armies of callers, and they will tell you anything to make you buy the stocks. Beware!

All of this is not to say that there are no low-priced legitimate stocks on the market. There are. They are usually small grassroots companies that can grow over time—if you pick the right one and wait a while. You should invest cautiously and conservatively at first. Look for a new company with good leadership in an industry where you see growth potential. It's also advantageous to find a company that holds the patent on a new product. If the product takes off, so could your stock. You must actively seek out all of this information—it will not come to you via a cold caller.

MUTUAL FUNDS

We're All in This Together

When you're first starting out with investing, it's hard to afford enough different stocks to have a diverse portfolio. Enter the mutual fund: a single investment for you that holds hundreds, or even thousands, of other investments. It offers you instant diversification and pieces of hundreds of companies for a much more manageable investment on your part. Think $3,000 rather than $300,000.

A mutual fund works like a basket of securities, a ready-made portfolio. Plus, there are many kinds of mutual funds, investing in everything from blue chip stocks to start-ups to government bonds. And while mutual funds do not trade over any stock exchange, they can have an enormous impact on the stock market itself.

HOW MUTUAL FUNDS WORK

Mutual funds gather money from huge numbers of investors and use that money to buy a portfolio of investments. Each individual investor in the mutual fund owns a portion of the whole portfolio, and indirectly a share of the many different assets it includes.

Mutual funds are bought and sold directly to and from the mutual fund company that issued them, even if you go through a broker or other financial professional for the transaction. They typically require minimum investments ranging from $1,500 to $5,000 to buy in. And mutual funds trade only once a day, after the markets have closed and that day's price can be determined. Mutual fund share prices are based on the net asset value (NAV) of the investments they hold.

DIFFERENT TYPES OF STOCK FUNDS

Mutual funds generally fall into one of two main categories: index funds and managed funds. Index funds, also called passive funds, closely track a specific stock index like the S&P 500, for example. Since the fund just mimics the makeup of its associated index, no active management is required. Managed funds seek to outperform various indexes by actively trading securities to "beat the market."

Within both of those categories, you'll find different types of stock funds that focus on a particular goal or piece of the market:

- Growth: stocks with potential for soaring share prices
- Income: stocks that pay regular dividends
- Value: stocks that seem like bargains when their price is compared to their true worth
- Sector: funds that zero in on companies in a particular market segment like technology or manufacturing
- International: funds that include stocks from countries outside the US
- Emerging markets: funds that seek out investments in developing countries
- Capitalization: funds that focus on only small-, mid-, or large-cap stocks

The array of options gives you the opportunity to invest in virtually any type of fund you want for a well-rounded stock portfolio.

UNDERSTAND ALL THE FEES AND EXPENSES

All mutual funds come with at least some fees and expenses, some much larger than others. Every dime that goes toward these reduces your returns. Plus, you'll pay those costs whether the fund makes or loses money, so in a period of losses you'll end up losing even more. That's why it's so important to know the total costs associated with your mutual fund investment. Common fees include loads (similar to sales commissions), redemption fees, exchange fees, account fees, management fees, and 12b-1 fees (or fund overhead costs, like marketing and shareholder services). Plus, when choosing among mutual funds, comparing their fees and expenses can help you make the best decisions for your portfolio.

Mutual Funds by the Numbers

Americans have $22.1 trillion invested in mutual funds, and those funds collectively hold 33% of total stocks on the market. There are 7,310 different mutual funds in all, including 4,332 that primarily invest in stocks.

HOW TO EVALUATE MUTUAL FUNDS

Once you know what types of mutual funds you want to invest in, you still have to pick individual funds. With literally thousands of funds to choose from, it can feel overwhelming to figure out which ones you want to buy. Most brokerage firms offer free online screening tools to help whittle down the options, but you still need to know which factors matter most to you and how to evaluate the results. Here are four factors to consider when deciding which funds to add to your portfolio:

1. Prioritize no-load funds so more of your money can go to work for you. Sales loads can carve a big chunk out of your investments, taking a long-term toll on earnings and growth potential. For example, if you make a $3,000 investment with a 5% load, you'll be losing $150 right off the bat. And over the long haul, you'll also lose all the compound earnings that $150 could have produced.
2. Look for funds with low expense ratios. When comparing two similar funds, the one with the lower expenses means higher returns. While the difference may seem small, 0.10% compared to 0.35% for example, it can add up to thousands of dollars over time.
3. Avoid funds with high turnover ratios, which let you know how often the securities held in the mutual fund get bought and sold. Since every sale inside the fund could create a taxable event for you, higher turnover means a potentially higher tax bill.
4. Check out the portfolio manager. With managed funds, the person making the investment choices matters a lot. Look at their bio, education, and experience. Then dig into their actions as the fund manager, such as how often they buy and sell securities, loss history, and track record for any funds they've ever managed.

You can find out more about any mutual fund by reading its prospectus, which you can find on the fund family's website. You can also look at independent online screening tools on sites like

Morningstar (www.morningstar.com) and the FINRA Fund Analyzer (www.finra.org).

HOW MUTUAL FUNDS AFFECT THE STOCK MARKET

Mutual funds hold about a third of the US stocks, so everything they do—buying, selling, holding shares—has an outsized effect on the stock market. Since their investments are so large, they have an impact on both short- and long-term stock prices and market activity.

Any time a mutual fund trades stock shares, it can trigger market trends. For example, if a fund decides to dump all of its holdings in ZZZ Corp., the price of ZZZ Corp. shares could drop, possibly significantly. That's partly due to the fund shares being sold, but also to the market's reaction. When one fund manager decides to divest, other fund managers may do the same, often followed by individual investors trying to ditch the stock as well. The reverse holds true as well: If a fund buys a large stake in a particular company, the share price will increase. The fund's move can influence investor confidence, leading to a buying frenzy for that company's shares and driving the price up even further.

EXCHANGE-TRADED FUNDS

Stock Me If You've Heard This

Exchange-traded funds (ETFs) are similar to mutual funds in that they each hold a full portfolio of other investments. That's where the similarity ends. The most obvious difference between the two is the way ETFs trade: ETF shares are bought and sold on the stock exchange, hence the name. Plus, ETFs offer a more flexible and often cheaper and easier way for new investors to get started.

With nearly 3,000 ETFs to choose from, you can invest in practically any type of asset. So, no matter what type of investments you need to round out your portfolio, there's an ETF to fill that slot.

HOW ETFS WORK

Like mutual funds, ETFs invest in big baskets of securities, then sell shares of the whole basket to the public. This offers investors instant diversification in a single investment, minimizing the risk that would come with investing in individual stocks.

You buy and sell ETFs on the stock exchange, rather than directly from or to the fund company, the same way you would trade individual stocks. That means you can buy or sell any time the market is open. You can also use some of the order types you'd use when buying stocks, like market orders (at the market price) or limit orders (only at a predetermined maximum price).

ETFs come with no minimum investment requirements like there are with most mutual funds. You can buy single shares of ETFs, so you don't need a lot of money to get started. In fact, you only need enough to cover one share plus any related trading commissions or fees, and that can come to less than $50. If you work with an online broker or institution that offers commission-free ETFs, and there are several, it takes even less cash to begin building your portfolio.

INVEST IN YOUR INTERESTS WITH ETFSS

Every ETF holds entire baskets of securities. Most ETFs passively follow published indexes like the Dow Jones Industrial Average or the Russell 2000. Since there's an index for virtually every possible market segment, you can buy ETFs that invest in everything from US stocks to global regions to commodities to real estate.

ESG Funds

Environmental, social, and corporate governance (ESG) funds invest in companies that strive to improve the world through their corporate actions. Examples include companies that prioritize diversity, equity, and inclusion (DEI), employ practices to address climate change, and focus on all of their stakeholders rather than just their stockholders.

While there's no lack of standard stock and bond index ETFs, you can also find specialty ETFs that allow you to invest in the things that most interest you. For example, you'll find ETFs that focus their holdings on video games, space exploration, luxury goods (like high-end watches and designer clothing), travel, ESG (environmental, social, and corporate governance), and precious metals.

These specialty (or niche) ETFs typically have active management and may charge higher fees than index-based ETFs.

ETFs by the Numbers

There are 2,934 ETFs in the US holding a combined $7.57 trillion of assets. Among those are 1,413 that hold US stocks, 769 invested in international stocks, 752 that hold other types of securities (such as bonds or commodities). More than 16 million American households have at least some money invested in ETFs.

HOW TO INVEST IN ETFS

Once you've decided to invest in ETFs, it's time to figure out which ones you want to add to your portfolio and buy them. Your first step will be to open and fund a brokerage account if you don't have one already. As you're choosing a brokerage, look for one that offers fee-free (or commission-free) trades for ETFs, such as Fidelity (www.fidelity.com) and Charles Schwab (www.schwab.com).

When you're ready to invest you'll decide which types of ETFs you're interested in: broad stock market funds, market sector funds, or dividend ETFs, for example. Once you've narrowed down the category you can begin to compare the individual funds. Here are five factors to consider when comparing ETFs:

1. **Look at the holdings.** Just because two ETFs track the same index doesn't mean they hold the exact same portfolio. Individual holdings may be weighted differently. For example, two different S&P 500 ETFs may both hold shares of Apple, but one may hold a higher percentage than another. ETFs generally disclose their holdings daily, so you can see what you're actually getting.
2. **Look at the tracking difference.** ETFs essentially track indexes (except for the very few that are actively managed). So, their returns should match—or at least be close to—the index returns. For example, if the S&P 500 has one-year returns of 12%, an ETF tracking the S&P 500 should have a similar return. The ETF return will typically be slightly lower due to fund expenses. But if it's much lower, consider a different ETF tracking the same index.
3. **Look at the asset level.** Size makes a difference when it comes to ETFs. Focus on funds that hold at least $10 million in assets, as smaller ETFs tend to generate less investor interest. That can make it harder to sell when you're ready.
4. **Look at costs.** There are two main types of costs associated with ETFs: trading commissions and expense ratios. Trading commissions typically run from $6 to $20 per transaction, but some brokerages offer commission-free ETF trades. ETF expense ratios also tend to be low, with the industry average under 0.5%.
5. **Look at trading volume.** You want an ETF that trades a lot of shares every day. That improves the fund's liquidity—how easy it will be for you to convert your shares back into cash. Smaller funds, extremely niche funds, and newer funds may have lower trading volume than larger, established funds.

You can find out more about any ETF by reading its prospectus, which you can find on the fund family's website. Most also have fact sheets online and make disclosures of their holdings readily available.

ETFS AND TAXES

When it comes to taxes, ETFs have an advantage over mutual funds. When ETFs generate and redeem shares, it doesn't result in a taxable transaction for investors. You'll only have to deal with taxes when you sell an ETF or earn interest and dividends.

The main tax associated with ETFs is capital gains tax, a special tax that applies when you sell assets for a profit. The amount of tax is based on how long you had the shares before you sold them: up to one year is a short-term capital gain, longer than one year is a long-term capital gain. Short-term capital gains get taxed at your normal income tax rate. Long-term capital gains get taxed at lower rates based on your income level and filing status.

Interest and dividends earned on ETFs are also subject to income tax. Many stock ETFs produce dividend income, while bond ETFs generate interest income. Both get taxed at your regular income tax rate.

REITS (REAL ESTATE INVESTMENT TRUSTS)

A Pocketful of Properties

Real estate investment trusts, or REITs (pronounced "reets"), give people the opportunity to invest in real estate for just a few hundred dollars or even less. It's the chance to own all kinds of rental properties without actually having to own or manage any buildings. REITs pool money from many investors to buy and hold income-producing real estate or real estate–adjacent investments, similar to how mutual funds hold stocks or bonds. While REITs earn income from a variety of sources, their main moneymaker is rental receipts.

Investing in REITs can help diversify a stock- or bond-heavy portfolio. Diversification helps reduce the overall risk factor of your portfolio. Plus, REITs often outperform the stock and bond markets, especially over long periods of time because their total return includes a combination of income and growth.

HOW REITS WORK

REITs must follow a unique set of strict requirements to enjoy their special tax status. To qualify as a REIT, the company must have at least 100 investors, earn at least 75% of its income from real estate (which includes real estate–related sources like mortgage loans), invest at least 75% of its assets in real estate and related sources, distribute 90% of its income directly to shareholders in the form of dividends, and have no more than half of its shares owned by five or fewer individuals.

Companies that meet all of the qualifications for a REIT get special tax treatment: They don't have to pay *any* taxes at the company level. That translates to more cash and higher returns for shareholders.

On the investor side, REITs work sort of like exchange-traded funds—shares of big baskets of real estate holdings that you can buy and sell just like stocks. When the REIT distributes income to you, you pay tax on it. You may also pay tax if you sell your REIT shares for more than you paid, creating a capital gain.

REITs by the Numbers

According to Nareit (the National Association of Real Estate Investment Trusts), publicly traded REITs hold more than 535,000 properties valued at nearly $3 *trillion* across the United States. They hold 15 million acres of timberland.

DIFFERENT TYPES OF REITS

There are three main types of REITs: equity, mortgage, and hybrid. The vast majority of REITs fall into the equity category, but all three are available to investors.

Equity REITs own, operate, and develop real estate assets such as apartment buildings, medical centers, and warehouses, with most of their income coming from rents received. They're classified by the type of real estate they hold. Retail REITs are the largest equity segment, making up about 17% of that market, and hold properties like malls, grocery stores, and boutiques. Other segments of equity REITs include:

- Residential: single and multifamily rental properties, retirement communities, and student housing
- Healthcare: hospitals, doctors' offices, and assisted-living facilities
- Office: office parks and office buildings
- Industrial: warehouses and distribution centers
- Self-storage: self-storage facilities
- Infrastructure: telecommunications towers and gas and oil pipelines
- Gaming: casinos, resorts, and gaming companies

Mortgage REITs, or mREITs, invest in the debt side of real estate. They can buy existing mortgages, invest in mortgage-backed securities, or act as direct mortgage lenders. They earn their income mainly through interest on the loans they hold, all of which are secured by actual real estate. Like other REITs, mREITs pass their income through to shareholders.

Hybrid REITs hold a combination of physical properties and mortgages. Their earnings come from both rental receipts and interest.

THE BENEFITS OF REIT INVESTING

Adding REITs into the mix can benefit your portfolio in a number of ways. That's why these securities are popular among wealthy and sophisticated investors. First, these income-heavy securities can provide passive income and regular cash flow. Second, they add an extra asset class to help diversify your investments. Third, REITs have a solid history of steady returns and long-term appreciation, with total returns that have outperformed the S&P 500 over the last twenty years. Fourth, REITs bring liquidity to a traditionally illiquid asset class, as you can cash out REIT shares whenever you want but it can take weeks, months, or years to sell physical real estate.

The main appeal, though, is that REITs give everyone inside access to big-ticket real estate deals: You can buy shares of a thriving industrial REIT for under $500, but you can't participate in a multimillion-dollar commercial real estate deal without having millions in the bank.

Of course, like all investments, REITs come with drawbacks as well. Their share prices are quite sensitive to interest rate fluctuations, and that's especially true for mREITs. REIT values are also affected by housing bubbles, and plummet when the bubbles burst. Another potential downside: Because REITs are required to distribute at least 90% of their income, there's not much left to reinvest in new holdings, leading to less room for capital appreciation. Plus, REITs are actively managed, which can result in relatively steep management fees when compared to passive mutual funds and ETFs.

HOW TO INVEST IN REITS

Most REITs are traded over stock exchanges or through mutual funds and ETFs, making it very easy to start investing. In fact, more than 150 million Americans own REITs in their retirement accounts, even if they're unaware of that.

All you need to get started is an investment account and money to invest. Once you decide you want to buy REIT shares, you'll need to choose which ones. That starts with clarifying your investment goals and figuring out what fits best with your existing portfolio and time horizon. Next, you'll narrow down which type of REIT you want—equity, mortgage, or hybrid—and then choose a sector. For the broadest REIT portfolio, you might want to start with a REIT-based mutual fund or ETF.

If you decide that individual REITs are for you, you'll do a little homework. Just like with stocks, you can find up-to-date information and statistics for any publicly traded REIT online, including current price, dividend yields, growth trends, asset value, and management history.

Reliable information sources include Nareit (www.reit.com) and *Yahoo! Finance* (www.finance.yahoo.com). You can also visit the specific REIT's corporate website and click on the "investors" tab to find SEC filings, annual reports, management presentations, and credit profiles. Once you've decided which REITs you want, log in to your investment account or contact your broker or financial advisor to buy the shares.

Some REITs Trade Off the Exchanges

Some REITs don't trade over stock exchanges. Private and nonlisted public REITs can only be traded with the help of a financial advisor or broker, and only by investors who meet minimum suitability requirements. Both types of off-exchange REITs have higher investment minimums, generally starting at $2,500 or more.

CRYPTOCURRENCY

Digital Dollars

Cryptocurrency, as we know it now, first came on the scene quietly when Bitcoin was released as open-source code in 2009. It was launched by the mysterious Satoshi Nakamoto, a pseudonym still surrounded by secrecy and conjecture, with the revelation of blockchain technology for a new peer-to-peer currency. The first bitcoins were "mined": People had to solve incredibly complex and difficult math problems correctly to verify their transactions, resulting in a small amount of bitcoin.

What Is Blockchain?

Blockchain is a digital record book, or ledger, with no central server home. The information is decentralized and widely distributed throughout a network to record data in blocks. With this setup, no block can be changed after the fact—they're irreversible. Each block is stored on many servers, and they must all match exactly for the block to remain valid.

Now, there are more than 22,000 unique cryptocurrencies in existence. Some, like Bitcoin and Ethereum, are widely known and widely traded. Others languish in obscurity trying to capture a small piece of crypto market share. These currencies can be either traded like stocks or spent like money, and their asset status (whether they're money or securities) remains unclear. What is clear: Investors seem to love the volatile roller-coaster ride and the hope that they'll uncover the next big cryptocurrency.

HOW CRYPTO AFFECTS THE STOCK MARKET

Cryptocurrency is a risky investment and is not for the faint of heart. With wild price swings, tons of scams, and confusion about tax treatment, these volatile assets can affect the stock market and the economy as a whole. When the 2022 crypto bubble burst and cryptocurrency values plummeted, for example, the stock market reacted.

Generally, the stock market and the crypto market seem to move in sync, affected by the same economic factors. Originally people believed that crypto would act as a hedge against stock downturns, but these two assets seem to ebb and flow along the same cycles. They're not directly related, rather they're correlated.

INVESTING IN CRYPTO STOCKS

Investors looking to get a taste of crypto without actually assuming all the risks of owning coins can turn to crypto stocks. These are shares of the companies inside and integral to the cryptocurrency industry and include:

- Cryptocurrency exchanges like Coinbase (COIN) and SoFi Technologies (SOFI)
- Payment platforms that facilitate using crypto, such as PayPal (PYPL) and Shopify (SHOP)
- Bitcoin mining companies, such as Marathon Digital (MARA) and Canaan (CAN)

- Blockchain companies, such as Riot Platforms (RIOT) and Hive (HIVE)
- Software or hardware development, such as Nvidia (NVDA) and Advanced Micro Devices (AMD)

These stocks tend to follow the crypto market: When crypto is up, their share prices rise and vice versa. As with any stocks you're interested in buying, find out everything you can about the corporation including its recent and historical performance and share price data. You'll also want to find information about how closely the stock correlates to crypto market performance, which will help you gauge how volatile the stock is likely to be.

CRYPTO FUNDS

First, let's address something there's a lot of confusion about: Crypto funds do not hold actual cryptocurrencies. They're not allowed to under current SEC guidelines (though that could change going forward). But that doesn't mean they aren't deep into crypto activity. Crypto ETFs and mutual funds do hold and trade crypto futures, sophisticated investment vehicles that essentially bet on the future prices of specific cryptocurrencies.

As of September 2023, there's only one crypto mutual fund: ProShares' Bitcoin Strategy ProFund. The fund has been live since July 2021 and holds Bitcoin futures, attempting to mimic Bitcoin's market pricing. The fund charges a relatively high expense ratio of 1.15% and requires a $1,000 minimum investment.

The ETF landscape is broader with several options for investors to choose from. These funds also invest in crypto futures contracts, tracking the pricing of the underlying coins. Until September 2023, crypto ETFs covered only Bitcoin, but then Ether (Ethereum) ETFs came on the scene.

On the pro side, these crypto funds give you access to an exciting asset class without the expense and hassles of direct ownership. On the con side, the options are limited, and no mutual funds or ETFs currently hold baskets of various cryptocurrencies, limiting investor exposure to just one or two cryptocurrencies.

There is one other fund type that does hold actual cryptocurrencies. These publicly traded Bitcoin investment trusts give investors indirect ownership in crypto, and all the risk and volatility that comes with it. Though these are technically publicly traded, shares are usually only available to institutional and accredited investors.

Are NFTs the Same As Crypto?

People often confuse cryptocurrencies and NFTs since both are digital assets, but the two are not the same. NFTs are non-fungible tokens, meaning they're unique and not interchangeable or duplicated. Cryptocurrencies are fungible, meaning one coin is the same as another, sort of like nickels or dimes, so it doesn't matter which specific coin you have.

BEWARE OF SCAMS

The cryptocurrency arena is fraught with fraud. It's already considered to be a speculative, risky asset class. Prices swing wildly even for the most stable coins. That makes it even easier for con artists and scammers to convince investors to part with their money...and never get it back.

The most common crypto scams include:

- Phishing for access to crypto wallets (devices or apps that store the keys that let you access your cryptocurrency).
- Fraudulent coins or tokens, where scammers impersonate established companies claiming to issue new cryptocurrencies.
- Rug pull scams, where crypto developers hype a new project, luring investors in with promises of huge returns, only to suddenly disappear with all of the investors' money (essentially pulling the rug out from under them).
- Pig butchering scams, where scammers initiate connections on social media or dating apps, take the time to build up a trusting relationship, and then convince their victims to buy cryptocurrency through a fake website.

Most of these scams relate to investing directly in cryptocurrencies, but some apply to crypto stocks as well. The takeaway: Do your research before you invest in anything.

DIVIDENDS

Money for Nothing

When a corporation is operating profitably and ends a fiscal period with plenty of cash on hand, its directors need to decide what to do with that money. They could choose to reinvest the surplus cash in the business, hoping to spur further profits. They could decide to pay down the corporate debt, or buy up another company. In many cases, though, successful corporations opt to share their windfalls with their shareholders. When they do distribute that extra cash to their investors, they are paying out dividends.

Dividends are payments made to shareholders that have nothing to do with stock price. These payouts are made simply because the company has reaped healthy profits and chooses to reward its shareholders. The corporate board of directors will decide whether and how often to pay a dividend to shareholders based on just how profitable the company is and how much cash they have on hand.

Dividends are usually more important to investors looking for income, and stocks that regularly pay dividends are thus known as income stocks. Many established companies pay dividends on a quarterly basis, and special one-time dividends may also be paid under certain circumstances.

When a company decides to pay dividends, the payout is based on its shares outstanding. The term "shares outstanding" refers to the number of shares a company has issued to the general public, including its employees. More shares outstanding can mean smaller dividends per shareholder; there's only so much money to go around, after all.

TRACKING DIVIDENDS

Before buying a stock for the dividends it's paying today, take a look at the dividends it's paid in the past. Compare the current dividend with the dividends paid over the past five years. Shrinking dividends may indicate plans for expansion; when a company's primary goal is growth, dividends may be small or nonexistent. To decide if a specific dividend stock makes sense for your portfolio, it's a good idea to compare it to other dividend stocks using the dividend yields.

The dividend yield converts the dollar value of an annual dividend (whether it's paid in cash or shares) into a percentage, allowing you to see the return rate. To compute the dividend yield, divide the annual dividend per share by the stock's share price. For example, if a corporation pays out a dividend of $0.50 per share, and the stock is trading at $25 per share, the dividend yield would equal 2% (0.50 ÷ 25 = 0.02).

DIVIDEND DATES

When it comes to reaping the benefits of a successful corporate year, shareholders need to pay attention to four very important dates:

1. Declaration date
2. Ex-dividend date
3. Date of record
4. Payable date

Corporations set these dates to make sure the right person receives the dividend check, and with stocks trading constantly, that can be a daunting task. So, if you are buying or selling a stock that comes with a dividend payout, make sure you know your dates.

The declaration date is the day the corporate board of directors announces that a dividend will be paid. This typically comes in the form of a public announcement, such as a press release, and possibly direct notification to shareholders (which now is typically done by email).

The ex-dividend date (sometimes also called the ex-date) is very important for people trading a stock for which a dividend has been declared. On and after the ex-dividend date, the stock trades without the dividend; if you buy a stock during this period, you will not receive the declared dividend. The ex-dividend date falls two days before the date of record.

Ticker Trivia

The ex-dividend date is necessary because there's a time lag between the day you buy a stock and the day the corporation records you as a shareholder.

The date of record is the day on which the corporation figures out exactly who gets the dividend checks. Only the shareholder of record on that day will receive the dividend payout.

As you might expect, the payable date refers to the day the dividend checks are mailed to the shareholders of record. This date often falls about a week after the date of record.

STOCK DIVIDENDS

Sometimes, instead of paying out dividends in cash, a corporation will reward its stockholders by issuing shares of stock as dividends.

This can happen when a corporation has positive earnings, but is short on cash or wants to use its cash reserves for another purpose.

Stock dividends are paid out of a corporation's treasury stock, which refers to shares of its own stock that the corporation holds. If the corporation doesn't have any treasury stock, it cannot pay out a stock dividend.

Here's how it works: Let's say QXZ Corporation had a stellar year and wants to pay dividends to its shareholders. There isn't enough cash stockpiled to pay everyone, but QXZ has treasury stock on hand. So QXZ opts to issue 0.05 dividend shares for each share a stockholder owns. If you owned 500 shares of QXZ, you would receive twenty-five new shares as your dividend.

If you happened to end up with any fractional shares, those would normally be paid out as cash. For example, if you owned 525 shares of QXZ, and the company declared a 0.05 stock dividend, your stock dividend would be 26.25 shares. Since you cannot trade a quarter of a share, you would get cash instead.

DRIPS

For investors who like the idea of earning dividends but don't need the cash, dividend reinvestment plans, known as DRIPs, will help their investments grow more quickly. Many companies that pay regular dividends offer these plans so that stockholders can automatically reinvest their dividends in extra shares.

Dividend reinvestment plans offer shareholders a simple and inexpensive way to purchase stock directly through a company, without having to pay commissions. This type of investment plan does not require the services of a broker. Such plans enable investors to purchase small amounts of common stock right from the corporation itself—in many cases, as little as $25 worth of stock at a time. Depending on the company, there may be a small fee for handling your account. In most cases, you will have to already own at least one share of the stock (purchased through a broker) to be eligible to participate in the DRIP. And, as the name implies, this plan only works for stocks that pay regular dividends, which must be reinvested in the stock.

Consider this: If you received cash dividends but really wanted more shares in the company, you would take that cash and buy more stock. A DRIP does that for you, effortlessly. Every dollar of dividend you'd be entitled to is transformed into more shares, every time they pay out dividends.

To find out whether a company offers a DRIP, look at the investor relations section on the corporate website.

Keep in mind that, as with all dividend earnings, there will be a tax bill at the end of the year. Even though you don't actually receive any money (since your dividends are used to get you more stock), you will have to pay taxes on any dividends you earned. Along those lines, it's critical that you keep very good records of your DRIP account. When the time comes for you to sell shares, you'll need to know exactly how much money you've paid for them, including your reinvested dividends. That way you will be able to accurately calculate the capital gain (or loss) at the time of the sale.

STOCK SPLITS

Two Are Better Than One

A stock split works in virtually the same way as breaking a twenty-dollar bill, changing that one bill for two ten-dollar bills. You'd still have the same amount of money, $20, but now you would have two bills instead of one. The mechanics of a stock split work just like that. In a two-for-one stock split, for example, each shareholder would get two shares for each single share he held before, and the price of each share would be split in half. The corporation increases the total number of its shares on the market without changing its total market capitalization.

Let's look at some numbers:

Suppose Spenser Corporation has 20 million shares outstanding, and the current share price is $30 per share, for a total market capitalization of $600 million (20 million shares × $30 per share). Spenser Corp. decides to execute a two-for-one stock split. Now there will be 40 million shares outstanding, and the per-share price will drop to $15. The total market capitalization hasn't changed at all: 40 million shares at $15 each still equals $600 million.

So if the market capitalization has not changed at all, why would a corporation bother to enact a stock split?

REASONS FOR STOCK SPLITS

There are two main reasons a corporation would split its stock: to lower the share price or to increase the liquidity.

The most common reason for a stock split relates directly to the stock price. When a share price gets too high, fewer people can afford to invest in it, especially in standard 100-share lots. For example, if a stock was trading at $50 per share, you would need $5,000 to buy 100 shares. But if the stock split two-for-one, bringing the share price down to $25, you would only need $2,500 to buy 100 shares. That price drop opens up the stock to many more potential investors.

Share liquidity is another reason corporations decide to implement stock splits, though this is less common. More shares on the market can bring more investors to the stock, making trading easier. This boost to share liquidity can push the bid-ask spread down, which also benefits investors.

DIFFERENT WAYS TO SPLIT

Not all stock splits use that two-for-one ratio. Other very common splits are three-for-one and three-for-two. And while none of those ratios affect the total market capitalization, each affects the shareholder and the share price differently.

Continuing the previous example, let's say Spenser Corp. called for a three-for-one split. Now there would be 60 million shares outstanding (3 × the original 20 million shares), and the price per share would drop to $10 ($30 per share divided by 3).

REVERSE STOCK SPLITS

Just as the name implies, a reverse stock split is the opposite of a regular stock split. In a reverse stock split, a corporation reduces its total number of shares outstanding. This action is also sometimes called a share rollback or a stock consolidation.

Typically, corporations that engage in a reverse split divide their shares by five or ten: a one-for-five split or a one-for-ten split. In a one-for-ten split, for example, each shareholder would walk away with only one share for every ten shares they held before. However, that single share would now have a share price ten times higher than before.

Ticker Trivia

In some cases, reverse split ratios are very high, demanding fifty-for-one or 100-for-one shares.

Let's look at reverse split math. Suppose Brady Corporation had 10 million shares outstanding and was trading at $1 per share for a total market capitalization of $10 million. If Brady Corp. decided to initiate a one-for-ten reverse stock split, the original 10 million outstanding shares would shrink to 1 million shares, and the original $1 per share price would increase to $10 per share. And, just like with a traditional stock split, the market capitalization would remain unchanged.

Virtually all reverse stock splits come about because share prices have dropped too low for the corporation to maintain its exchange listing status. Under normal economic conditions, the major exchanges enforce a minimum share price of $4 for new listings, and $1 for companies that are already trading. Those rules have been suspended in times of deep economic trouble, like a sustained bear market.

MERGERS AND ACQUISITIONS

Let's Get Together

For hundreds of years, companies have come together through mergers and acquisitions. They do this primarily to increase shareholder value: Combining forces can provide a competitive edge, increasing the value of the resultant corporation for stockholders.

When two companies combine, whether through merger or acquisition, they can gain many potential advantages, such as better market share, reduced financial risk, cost savings, and increased profitability.

On the other hand, mixing two companies can also result in friction and conflict. Disparate corporate cultures can make it difficult for employees to work together efficiently. Integrating different computer systems, corporate processes, and business plans can lead to major sticking points as the new company goes through growing pains. In the worst cases, the new company cannot function effectively, and shareholders suffer as the stock price falls.

MERGERS

Mergers are deals where two companies come together as one, blending their businesses by mutual agreement of their boards of directors and with shareholder approval. Most commonly, when this happens, a new combined company is formed. Shareholders of each original company would now own shares in the newly formed company.

There are three basic types of mergers: horizontal, vertical, and circular.

A horizontal merger involves the blending of two companies in the same industry. Before they combined, the two companies were competitors, selling the same products to the same customers. After they join forces, they consolidate their businesses into one stronger, more competitive corporation. The new larger company can be more profitable due to improved economies of scale. That means they can lower costs based on increased volume, similar to buying in bulk at the grocery store. Meta, the blending of Facebook and Instagram, was an example of a horizontal merger.

In a vertical merger, two corporations that operate in different parts of the same business come together. Typically, each contributes different services or physical goods toward the same end product, like a soda manufacturer and a sugar producer both play a role in bringing soft drinks to the grocery store. The basic idea behind a vertical merger is to bring together companies that can operate more effectively as one company. With sugar now in-house, the soda manufacturer can reduce the cost to make their soft drinks, and even possibly grow the business by supplying sugar to other food and beverage producers.

Circular mergers diverge widely from the other merger types. These combinations strive to bring a broader range of products and services to their customers, sometimes mixing quite disparate companies. These can be the riskiest types of mergers, especially if the companies joining forces don't really understand the business of the other. A circular merger could combine, for example, a makeup manufacturer with a soap and shampoo manufacturer.

Most mergers result in somewhat more successful corporations. Sometimes, though, the combination of two companies brings spectacular success, like Disney Pixar, where the market can hardly remember the separate companies that came before; other times, mergers can result in dismal failures.

EXXONMOBIL, A SUCCESSFUL MERGER

One of the most fruitful mergers in financial history happened back in 1999. Consistently low oil prices were plaguing the industry, and big oil corporations were looking for ways to turn the tide back toward exceptional profitability.

In this climate, Exxon and Mobil, two oil giants, agreed to merge. The deal went through for $81 billion, an amount critics and naysayers deemed too much, and Exxon Mobil Corporation was formed; at the time it was the largest corporation in the world. The combined forces of Exxon Mobil Corporation (XOM) thrived, and the deal remains one of the most successful mergers to ever grace the financial pages.

IMPACT ON SHAREHOLDERS

When two corporations plan to merge, both of their share prices begin to change unpredictably, causing a great deal of shareholder anxiety. Right before the deal is complete, share prices may spike or dip. Once that roller-coaster ride comes to an end, shareholders of both original companies can expect shares in the newly formed company to be higher.

In addition to price changes, shareholders can expect some differences in their voting power. With more shares outstanding after the merger, stockholder positions may be diluted. This is especially common with stock-for-stock mergers, where the new company hands out shares in exchange for shares of the former companies at a preset conversion rate (which is not always one for one).

ACQUISITIONS

Acquisitions take place when one company buys another. The acquiring company absorbs the target company into its business. Though acquisitions, sometimes called friendly takeovers, may be done at the agreement of the companies (as happens in a merger), one now owns the other. Unlike a merger, no new company emerges.

To acquire a target company, the purchasing company buys up a majority share of the target firm's stock, often paying a tidy premium to existing shareholders. Neither company changes its name, and no new company shares are issued; both companies carry on as before, except that now the acquiring company owns the target corporation.

Ticker Trivia

A management acquisition occurs when a member of a corporation's current management team buys up a controlling interest in the company, basically turning it into a private corporation. These deals often involve a lot of debt financing, and require the approval of a majority of shareholders in order to go through.

IMPACT ON SHAREHOLDERS

When one corporation acquires another, that action affects the shareholders of both companies, but in very different ways. On top of that, the way the acquiring company purchases the target company stocks can alter the effects on shareholders.

When the acquiring company uses money to get the target company's stock, the share price of each company changes. Right before the transaction is finalized, the share price of the acquiring company normally drops. This dip is typically temporary, and the share price rebounds once the deal has gone through. On the other side, the stock price of the target company rises, because the acquiring company typically pays a premium to buy those shares.

But money is not the only way an acquiring company can purchase another firm. Stocks can be used too. With a stock-for-stock transaction, the acquiring firm trades its stock for shares in the target firm. This then gives the target company's shareholders a stake in the acquiring company. For example, when ABC Corp. attempts to acquire XYZ Inc., it could offer current XYZ stockholders one share of ABC for every two shares of XYZ they own.

Further, acquisitions can also be done using a combination purchasing strategy: using a mix of stock and cash to obtain shares of the target company. For example, ABC could offer XYZ stockholders one share of ABC plus $5 for each share of XYZ they hold. This combined approach is the most common way acquisitions take place.

As for voting power, that will change for both sets of shareholders after the acquisition is finalized. While both will likely see their power diluted somewhat, shareholders of the target firm are usually impacted more. Especially with a stock-for-stock acquisition, which requires the issuance of additional shares, the proportion of shares any stockholder owns will shrink. For example, an ABC shareholder who previously owned a 3% stake in the company may see her holdings diluted to 2.25% after the issuance of the additional shares required to acquire XYZ.

DEALS DON'T ALWAYS WORK OUT

Most mergers and acquisitions are successful. Sometimes, though, deals fall through. This can happen for a few different reasons:

- One or both parties withdraw from the deal
- A regulatory body prohibits the deal
- The acquiring company can't find adequate financing
- Skeletons in the target company's closet are uncovered

It's not unusual for a company to put out feelers for mergers or acquisitions, then get cold feet. For example, change in board members or upper management can alter the company's direction and momentum, nixing plans for a potential combination. Shareholder resistance, economic shifts, and market swings can also affect upcoming deals.

When a prospective corporate merger or acquisition violates state or federal law, a regulatory body will come in and nix the deal. Most often, this happens when the new combination brushes up against antitrust or monopoly regulations. Written to protect consumers, these regulations strive to ensure market competition. Mergers or acquisitions that would create monopolies or severely limit competition for a particular industry are not allowed, but that doesn't mean that corporations don't try to slide such transactions through.

Funding issues are much more common with acquisitions than with mergers. When one corporation sets out to buy another, it has to purchase the takeover target's stock from current shareholders, always at an enticing premium over market price. These deals can run into billions of dollars, and acquiring companies can't always come up with the financing in time to see the deal through. In that case, the acquiring company withdraws from the transaction, and the deal does not go through.

Sometimes when an acquiring firm begins to dig deep into a target company's books, irregularities or hidden losses get uncovered. Under the skeptical eye of an ace accountant, for example, creative bookkeeping can come to light. The activity may not necessarily constitute illegal book cooking, but there may be inventive interpretations of the rules that cause profits to look bigger than they would be under more traditional accounting methods. Or perhaps the target company hasn't been fully forthcoming about unsuccessful research and development projects, potential lawsuits or scandals, or other deal-breakers that the acquirer discovers during due diligence. Damaging skeletons in corporate closets can kill takeover transactions, if they're uncovered.

HOSTILE TAKEOVERS

Pirates Plunder the SS *Megabucks*

When a firm that is targeted for acquisition opposes the buyout attempt, it's called a hostile takeover. These deals can get downright nasty, as corporate raiders battle a resistant management team and board of directors. The enmity trickles down to the target firm's employees, stoking their loathing of the corporate conqueror and their expectations of getting fired in the aftermath. This pervasive animosity makes it almost impossible for the target of a hostile takeover to thrive after the deal is done.

Because it can be such a combative process, corporate raiders may sneak up on target companies. One example of this is the "dawn raid" maneuver. In this ambush, the investor (which can be a person or a company) stays under the radar, sending out buy orders for target company shares to various brokers, with instructions to purchase the stock at the opening bell. This strategy has a dual impact. The identity of the raider is hidden behind the brokers, so the target company board doesn't know who hit them. Because the stealth transaction takes place first thing, the company won't hear about the massive buy-up until it's too late. Plus, since the market doesn't have time to react and drive up the share price, the raider scoops up shares at the current price.

Another type of sneak attack that used to be more popular, until the US government put a damper on it, is called the "Saturday night special." This strategy gets its name from the fact that the move is initiated over a weekend. This plot involves a public tender offer, where the acquiring party announces a willingness to buy shares at a premium. Their aim is to snap up a controlling interest before the target company has time to react. This scheme lost favor after the Williams Act was passed in 1968. The act basically requires that any corporate stock acquisition of 5% or more must be reported to the SEC.

BREAKING DOWN THE WILLIAMS ACT

The Williams Act was passed by Congress in 1968 to make sure that neither target companies nor their shareholders could be ambushed by an unwanted takeover. Under this law, the acquiring company is required to disclose their plans to the SEC and provide shareholders with a full disclosure.

As soon as any party acquires 5% of a corporation's shares, this act kicks in. When it does, the acquirer must report:

- The source of the funds being used to take over the target company
- The reason they want to buy the company
- What they plan to do with the company once they have a controlling interest
- Any contracts or agreements they have in place with the target company

Unfortunately, unscrupulous raiders find ways around this well-intentioned act. They can skirt the law by using derivative securities, like stock options, to accomplish their goals.

Whatever tactics they use to gobble up shares in the target company, the parties initiating a hostile takeover must have a lot of resources on hand. No matter what strategy they employ, the acquiring party almost always ends up paying more than the market price to garner a controlling interest.

In response to these underhanded stock grabs, target corporations have developed their own brand of tricks designed to keep raiders away. Those strategies fall under the category of shark repellent, and include imaginative tactics like poison pills, golden parachutes, and sandbags, which will be discussed later in more detail.

CORPORATE RAIDERS

Like the Vikings plundering village treasures, corporate raiders attack asset-rich corporations in an attempt to acquire them through a hostile takeover bid. But it takes more than a desire to pillage to become a successful corporate raider; it takes a lot of funding and a strong stomach.

To acquire his target, the raider tries to buy up enough shares of the corporation to gain a controlling interest. Because he doesn't have the approval of the target company's board of directors, he has to circumvent them. If he can't grab enough shares to succeed, the raider may appeal directly to the company's shareholders, asking them to sell their shares for a premium.

Despite their zeal for snapping up shares and adding corporations to their holdings, raiders typically don't intend to keep the companies they acquire. Rather, these calculating businesspeople look to make enormous, quick profits by chopping the companies up and selling off their valuable assets. For that reason, they zero in on corporations that have undervalued assets, meaning that what the target company owns is worth more than the market realizes.

For example, let's say Big Money Corporation has a million shares on the market with a current stock price of $10, for a total $10 million market value. To keep things simple, suppose Big Money has no debt and a lot of cash on hand, $2 million, and other assets on the books totaling $8 million. The market value of those assets, though, is currently $15 million. That would make Big Money Corporation desirable prey for a corporate raider, because the company's assets are undervalued by $5 million.

BARBARIANS AT THE GATE

Spurred by unbridled arrogance and insatiable greed, one larger-than-life CEO set out to line his pockets by wielding his corporate power. This true-life drama inspired the 1993 film *Barbarians at the Gate*, but the real story eclipses the fictional plot.

The story begins back in the 1980s, when cigarettes were attracting more lawsuits than new smokers. R.J. Reynolds Tobacco Company came under pressure and was facing a very precarious future. Conservative and cost-conscious CEO J. Tylee Wilson began to put out feelers for a potential merger. After careful consideration and a lot of advice, Wilson landed on Nabisco Brands, led by F. Ross Johnson, the villain of our tale.

Johnson had come from Standard Brands, where under his reign as CEO his salary tripled, and corporate jets and luxury cars were added to the executive perks, all with the approval of the board. Standard Brands merged with Nabisco back in 1981, creating Nabisco Brands, and Johnson soon found himself, once again, in the top spot, where he promptly set out to curry favor among the board members. Then, once again, he used the corporate checkbook to fund his lavish lifestyle and line his personal pockets, with no objections from the board.

The two disparate executives finally met in the spring of 1985 to discuss the merger they both wanted. With a much longer and stronger background, Wilson intended to act as chairman of the newly formed company with Johnson his second in command. Johnson wasn't really interested in being a vice chairman, opting instead for a more active role in the corporation as its president and COO. The deal finally went through, with R.J. Reynolds buying Nabisco Brands for a record-breaking $4.9 billion (the largest amount ever paid for a non-oil company at the time). As Wilson and Johnson began to work together at RJR Nabisco, their contrasting styles became quickly apparent. Johnson, in his usual style, cozied up to the board members, and began to turn them against Wilson. In less than one year, Johnson was top dog and enjoying a huge salary with lavish perks.

Then, in 1987, RJR Nabisco stock suffered a one-two punch. The market crash hit their share price hard, and at the same time tobacco products were falling out of favor with consumers. Always looking out for himself, Johnson started to search for new ways to bring in money that wouldn't involve anyone looking over his shoulder. Interested in the benefits of a leveraged buyout or LBO (which is where one company buys another with mostly borrowed money), Johnson connected with expert Henry Kravis from KKR (Kohlberg Kravis & Roberts), who was very interested in pursuing the deal to buy RJR Nabisco. At the same time, behind his back, Johnson was secretly working with another investment bank, Shearson Lehman Hutton. In this deal, Johnson insisted on receiving 20% of the company stock (for himself and some other top management personnel) and complete control of the board, virtually the definition of a black knight attempting a hostile takeover.

A bidding battle broke out between KKR (who wanted nothing more to do with Johnson) and Shearson Lehman Hutton (still working with Johnson). First came a bid for $75 a share from Johnson's team, then $90 from KKR, and the bids climbed higher and higher as RJR Nabisco board members watched. All of a sudden, a gray knight appeared; out of nowhere, First Boston bid $118 per share. But when the financing for that fell through, the board decided to accept KKR's $109 per share bid even though it was slightly lower than the bid from Shearson Lehman Hutton. The deal finally closed for another record-breaking amount, $25 billion.

KKR kicked Johnson out of his post at the company, but Johnson still won in the end. As part of his contract, Johnson walked away with his golden parachute intact, leaving RJR Nabisco with $30 million.

KNIGHTS OF MANY COLORS

In a medieval twist, some parties to takeovers are known as knights. Just like in old tales of castles, princesses, and round tables, the black knights are the bad guys. Here, these corporate raiders seek to take over a resistant company that does not want to be bought in what is known as a hostile takeover attempt.

White knights ride in to the rescue, offering the target company a way out of the hostile takeover. This corporate savior gives the company a chance for a friendly takeover instead.

A yellow knight starts out as a black knight, attempting a hostile takeover. Midway through the process, this party switches up his strategy and begins to negotiate with the target company, hoping to resolve the matter to benefit both sides.

Sometimes when an acquiring party and a target company are in the middle of talks, a gray knight rides in with his own bid, out of the blue.

PROXY FIGHTS

An all-out battle among stockholders of the target company is called a proxy fight. Like other facets of hostile takeovers, proxy fights can get downright ugly.

Investors in favor of the takeover attempt to bring the other shareholders around to their side, persuading them to approve the action. They accomplish that by getting the shareholders' proxies: the right to act on behalf of those shareholders in an upcoming vote. If the raiding party scoops up enough proxies, they win, and the takeover goes through—even if the board of directors is opposed to it.

Companies concerned about potential takeover attempts may decide to issue different kinds of shares: some with fewer voting rights, and others with more voting rights. The shares with fewer voting rights may pay a higher dividend rate to make them more attractive to investors. These are called DVRs (differential voting rights). Holders of DVR shares may, for example, get one vote for every hundred shares they own. This strategy, which can make it more difficult for a raider to get enough votes, is gaining popularity among potential target corporations.

TENDER OFFERS

Sometimes a corporate raider will go directly to the source to buy target company stock: the current shareholders. In a move called a tender offer, the raider promises to buy their shares at a fixed price that's greater than the current market price.

For example, if shares in ABC Inc. were trading for $10 per share, the raider would pledge to pay ABC stockholders $12 per share if they sold directly to him. That $2 difference is the premium over market price, a cost of doing business for the corporate raider.

There is a catch, however. Enough shareholders must agree to the deal—enough to give the raider a controlling interest—or the sale will not go through.

GREENMAIL

Similar to blackmail, greenmail is used by a corporate raider to force a target company to buy back its own shares at highly inflated prices in order to prevent a hostile takeover. It begins with a corporate raider buying up target company shares, accumulating enough stock to become a viable threat.

Once the target company board realizes its position, the raider announces the greenmail demand. The target corporation is then forced to buy their shares from the raider, at a significant premium over the market price so that they can save their company, and thus thwart the takeover attempt.

SHARK REPELLENT

Corporate raiders act like pillagers, striking fat targets with the speed and precision of a shark. To fend them off, targeted companies need strong shark repellent. That is, they need a collection of strategies designed to deter even the most voracious predator.

Take the sandbag defense, for example. With this tactic, the target company tries to stall the raider, hoping to get a better offer from a more favorable party, called a white knight. The managers of a target company must strike a fine balance here, as they attempt to keep the raider at bay and entice a white knight to come to their rescue—all while they're still running the company.

Or consider the Pac-Man defense, where the target company turns the tables and gobbles up shares of the acquiring company. Another inventive tactic called the crown jewel defense involves the target company's most valuable assets. In the case of a hostile takeover, the corporate bylaws state that those most valuable assets must be sold, and the acquiring company would be legally forced to comply, selling off the very things it was after in the first place.

Poison Pills

In an attempt to thwart an impending hostile takeover, a target corporation may employ a poison pill strategy. This tactic is designed to make the company appear unattractive so that the raider loses interest. The tricky part: not making the company so unattractive that its share price never recovers (insiders call that situation a "suicide pill").

The two most common poison pill strategies are flip-in and flip-over, and each has a direct impact on the company's investors.

With a flip-in poison pill, the company's existing shareholders (other than the party attempting the takeover) can buy up more shares for a discounted price. This serves a dual purpose: weakening the acquirer's stock position and making the deal more painful and pricey for her. Suppose the acquirer has just obtained 5% of the outstanding shares. When the flip-in is enacted, more shares come onto the market. That dilutes her 5% holding and her power. On top of that, she now has to pick up even more shares to gain a controlling interest, making this a more expensive takeover than expected. This strategy is often included in the shareholder rights plan of the target corporation.

This poison pill tactic was implemented in 2022 by (then) Twitter to ward off the takeover by Elon Musk. When Musk announced that he had bought up almost 9% of the corporation's shares, Twitter quickly established a plan that prevented anyone from snapping up more than a 15% threshold without negotiating for a fair value. However, the company agreed to a buyout during April 2022, and in October Musk acquired Twitter—now X—for $44 billion.

Ticker Trivia

In the event of a hostile takeover, the "people pill" strategy calls for the walkout of key personnel.

The flip-over poison pill plan is less commonly used. This strategy lets the shareholders of the target company buy stock in the acquiring company for a bargain basement price. Since this provision is written into the target company's shareholder rights plan, the acquiring company has to honor it, even at the expense of its existing shareholders.

Golden Parachutes

Golden parachutes are among the most controversial forms of shark repellent. The strategy is designed to ward off potential raiders by promising extremely lucrative payouts to the current corporate bigwigs, executives like the CEO (chief executive officer) and CFO (chief financial officer). Often, these top dogs lose their positions in the event of a corporate takeover, and the golden parachute ensures they'll land softly when their jobs are gone.

Typically, golden parachutes are part of executive employment contracts. They can include benefits such as:

- Stock options
- Cash bonuses
- Huge severance packages
- Continuing perks (like company cars)
- Outplacement services

These golden parachutes often deliver millions of dollars' worth of benefits to those executives, and the acquiring company will be on the hook to pay them out, making the takeover target much more expensive.

Why the controversy? Golden parachutes reward top executives, often at the expense of the shareholders.

The Macaroni Defense

Another strategy an unwilling target company can employ to deter would-be takeover attempts is known as the macaroni defense. To accomplish this, the company issues bonds that come with a very special pledge: If the company is taken over, the bonds must be redeemed for even more money. Basically, in the case of a hostile acquisition, the corporate debt expands—in much the same way that macaroni expands when you throw it in boiling water. To really make an impact, though, the bond issue has to be large enough to scare off the raider.

The downside to the macaroni defense is increased debt and the expense of interest payments. Even when the tactic successfully stops a takeover, it leaves the target company saddled with this large new liability.

ESOPs

Another way to preempt a hostile takeover involves corporate forethought, and the implementation of an employee stock ownership plan, or ESOP. ESOPs are a type of retirement plan, like 401(k)s and other such plans, and an ESOP provides tax benefits for everyone involved.

When a corporation creates an ESOP, they give their employees stock in the company, stacking the deck against would-be corporate raiders. People who own a stake in the company they work for are far more likely to vote with familiar, trusted company management than with an invading outsider.

Thousands of publicly traded corporations employing millions of workers maintain ESOPs, and some of those companies are at least 50% owned by their employees. Examples include Publix Super Markets (based in Florida), with a roster of 250,000 employees, and Davey Tree Expert (based in Ohio), which boasts 11,460 employees in the United States.

BUYING AND SELLING

Rule No 1: Don't Lose Money

Most educators will tell you that 75% of all learning is gained by doing homework. This is true of investing as well. When you are interested in investing, it's important that you do your homework in the form of research, analysis, and investigation. Use the Internet to look up the stock you own and find any company news listings. Read the company newsletter, its annual or semiannual reports, and ask your broker for any updated news about the company. An educated investor is more likely to be a patient and relaxed investor.

BUY WHAT YOU KNOW

One of the benefits of being a consumer is that you are called on to evaluate products and services every day. You have learned that you can get the best results by thoroughly researching your options before you make a purchasing decision. Maybe you've recently purchased some new electronics that you just can't put down, switched cereal brands to cut some of the sugar out of your kids' diet, or started a new medication that actually made you feel better without any side effects. You can put your experiences as a savvy consumer to work when you're making your investment decisions.

Your observations are another way to gain valuable insight. During your recent trip to Japan, did you notice people consuming huge quantities of a new Coca-Cola product? While waiting to pay for dinner at your favorite restaurant, did you notice that many of the patrons pulled out American Express cards? Part of doing your homework as an investor is noticing the products and services that are prominently displayed and used by the people around you.

Another huge consideration when buying stocks is price. Would you pay any amount to buy a car or a house? Probably not. Most people like to feel that they've gotten a good deal. They're looking for a price that's proportionate to their buying budget and what they get from the purchase. It's the same with stock investing: The price of a particular stock is a critical part of the buying and selling equation. Taking a business attitude toward stock buying is important—it is wise to base your investment decisions on a variety of factors, including purchase price. That's the only way to ensure profitability in the long run. You want high quality at a fair (or better than fair) price.

Fortunately, good-quality companies in this country are plentiful. Finding these companies, however, is something of a challenge. Some investors are more inclined to look for the current hot stock, while others prefer to hunt out a great deal. Growth investing and value investing are two common approaches. (Earlier sections offer more detailed information about these approaches.)

GET THE FACTS

Both styles of investing can be lucrative. The idea is to figure out which style of investment better fits your personality and investment strategy. Sometimes you may lean toward growth investing; other times, you may feel that taking a value-investing approach is the way to go. Still other times you may want growth and value all wrapped up in one neat package. In that case, you would be looking for growth at a reasonable price, known in industry lingo as GARP.

Whichever style you choose, you need a place to get the information on which you can base your decision. These days, there's no better starting point than the Internet. On the web, you can easily find the best investment information in real time, mostly for free. More and more, investors both young and old are turning to websites to limit their reliance on expensive financial advisors. In addition to the prospect company's web page, there are dozens of sites that provide in-depth company data, and even more sites offer real-time stock quotes.

Checklist

Every investor should use a research checklist to evaluate stock under consideration. Look for annual reports, financial statements, industry comparisons, and current news items. Analyze your findings before making investment decisions. Once you become a shareholder, your information needs can be fulfilled with press releases, ongoing financial statements, and stock price monitoring.

There is no shortage of good market research available to you as an investor. Part of your job is to determine which sources work best.

TWO PROVEN WAYS TO ANALYZE STOCKS

Investors generally favor one of two stock-picking techniques: technical analysis or fundamental analysis. Technical analysis is all about stock prices and how they move, and it relies on charts and graphs to determine patterns. Fundamental analysis, more common among beginning investors, involves studying the company itself, with a focus on financial statements and performance. For optimum results, many savvy investors combine both techniques when making trade decisions. For example, a stock with great fundamentals and sagging price trends could indicate trouble on the horizon.

Technical analysis focuses on charts and graphs showing past stock prices and volume patterns. There are a number of patterns technical analysts recognize to be historically recurring. The trick is to identify the pattern before it is completed, and then buy or sell according to where the pattern indicates the stock is headed. Those who use this technique believe you can forecast future stock prices by studying past price trends. They make trades based primarily on stock price movements. Technical analysts tend to do much more buying and selling than fundamental analysts.

Fundamental analysis is a long-used, common way to review stocks. The technique involves an analysis of the company's ability to generate earnings and an examination of the value of the company's total assets. Value investing and growth investing are two subdivisions of fundamental analysis. Proponents of fundamental analysis believe that stock prices will rise as a result of growth. Earnings, dividends, and book values are all examined, and a buy-and-hold approach is usually followed. Advocates of fundamental analysis maintain that stock in well-run, high-quality companies will become more valuable over time.

KNOW WHEN TO SELL

Knowing when to hold and when to sell a particular stock is an art in itself. You may have every intention of sticking with your investments for the long haul, but maybe the first sign of turbulence sends you into a panic to sell. History has revealed that holding on to solid stocks for a minimum of five to ten years has produced the best results. Therefore, buying good companies and holding them for the long term is a sound strategy for most investors.

When you decided to buy your stock, you thoroughly researched its balance sheet, income statement, and ratio analyses. The same holds true when you're thinking of selling a stock. Before you jump on a sell bandwagon because of something you see on the news or hear at the water cooler, reevaluate your holdings carefully. If the share value is still growing, selling too soon can mean you will miss out on additional profits. At the same time, though, you don't want to hold on to a losing stock. Selling at the wrong time can easily destroy your investing plan, so don't do it on impulse. And don't worry about losing your shirt; there's a simple way to make sure that doesn't happen.

The primary way to lock in your profits and limit your losses is with a standing stop-loss order. A stop-loss order is a specialized instruction to your broker, either live or online, that tells them to sell a stock when its price has declined by a certain percentage. A stop loss can be placed based on the original buy price, or it can move with the stock price (called a trailing stop). Here's how it works: Suppose you buy a stock for $10 per share. You want to limit your losses to 10%. You would place a stop order for $9 per share, which means that if the share price fell to $9, your broker would automatically sell the stock.

With a trailing stop, the sell price increases proportionally when the stock price goes up, helping you both limit losses and lock in already earned profits. Suppose you bought that same $10 stock, and you want a 10% loss limit. When the stock goes up to $15.00, your trailing stop increases to $13.50, 10% less than the new share price.

EXECUTING STOCK TRADES

The Nuts and Bolts of Trading

As an individual investor in the stock market, your first concern is how to go about executing a stock trade. Fortunately, it's usually as simple as picking up the phone or clicking the mouse. For example, if you trade through a broker, you can simply call and place an order for 100 shares of any company, like Etsy or Disney. Almost immediately, you'll get confirmation that your order has been filled and that you now own stock in Etsy or Disney. When you make your own online trades, you simply follow the point-and-click instructions on the brokerage website to execute your trade. A confirmation should follow almost immediately.

Of course, things can get a little more complicated, as there are several different types of stock orders. Your options include a market order (like the Etsy or Disney example), a limit order, and a stop order (which includes a stop order buy, and a stop order sell). You can also determine the length of time your order is in effect. For example, you can specify that the order is only good for the specific day on which it is placed.

MARKET ORDER

When you want to buy or sell a stock at the current market price, you place a market order. This means you want to buy or sell a stock at whatever price the stock is trading for when your order reaches the floor. In other words, you're buying or selling a given stock at the going rate. Depending on whether you're buying or selling, the market price may differ. The broker's terms for these prices are the bid (buy) or ask (sell), and the difference between these two prices is known as the spread. For example, Etsy's bid price (the amount someone is willing to pay) may be $60.60, while its asking price (the amount someone is willing to accept) is $60.65. In this case, the spread is five cents.

A Good Price Barometer

Get an idea of the fifty-two-week highs and lows of the stocks you're looking to purchase and use this to set target prices for when to sell. As the stock approaches the target price you can start selling off shares, and then gauge to what degree you believe it might pass the target. Don't use the target as an absolute figure but as a barometer.

Unlike Etsy or Disney, securities that are thinly (infrequently) traded often have bigger spreads. Dealers in a security generally keep a large part of the spread in exchange for playing the role of middleman. Like all middlemen, dealers are in the business of selling goods at a higher price than what they initially paid. Stock prices, especially in heavily traded stock, can change in just seconds. By the time your order is filled with a market order, you might find a slight difference in the price you were quoted.

When you place the order, you can specify a particular time frame during which the trade can be executed. Standard order periods include:

- Day orders, which are either filled or automatically expire by the end of the trading day

- Minute orders, which expire as soon as the specified number of minutes have passed
- GTD (good-til-date) orders, which stay active until they are either filled or canceled
- GTC (good-til-canceled) orders, which stay open until they are executed or canceled
- AON (all-or-none) orders, which must be filled in their entirety or they get canceled at the end of the trading day
- FOK (fill-or-kill) orders, which have to be filled instantly and entirely or not at all
- IOC (immediate-or-cancel) orders, which are canceled if not filled instantly, either entirely or partially

These time frames can be applied to market orders and limit orders, and are used to give the investor more ways to control the execution of his stock trades.

LIMIT ORDER

Limit orders are placed if you don't want to purchase stock for more or sell a stock for less than a predetermined price. A limit order, like other types of orders, can be placed as a day order or as a GTC (good-til-canceled) order. Your limit order may not fill with either one of these two options. However, you have a greater chance of your order being filled with a GTC order since it can remain open for a longer period of time.

If you want to buy a stock for a specified price, you can place a limit buy order. Let's say Amazon.com (AMZN) is currently trading at $146. You want to buy 100 shares of Amazon, but only if it dips to $140. In this case, you place a limit order for 100 shares of Amazon at $140 per share. The order will fill for $140 per share if the price dips to that level (or lower). If it does not, your order will remain unfilled. Your order to buy stock may also be filled for less than $140 per share if the stock hits $140 and continues to drop. If that happens, your order would fill at the first available price under $140. This happens because prices often move more quickly than trades can be settled. One thing is for certain, though: Your order will not fill for more than $140 per share.

Now let's say you own stock in Amazon.com, and you bought it at $140 per share. To lock in profits, you might decide to place a limit order to sell your shares if the stock price climbs to $160 per share. In this case, your order will fill for at least $160 per share, though it could be filled for more than that amount if the stock price hits $160 and continues to rise. In this beneficial circumstance, your stock would be sold at the first opportunity at $160 or higher; again, stock prices usually move faster than sell orders can settle. However, your order to sell those Amazon.com shares will not fill for less than $160 per share.

Be aware, though, that brokers typically charge a higher commission to fulfill a limit order than to execute a market order. That offset can eat away at gains, so it's important to factor that in when setting limit prices.

STOP ORDER

Stop orders (also called stop-loss orders) are crucial for investors who are concerned about a stock's price falling too low, and want to lock in profits or limit losses. Using either a fixed dollar amount or a percentage, the investor sets a stop point; that is, a price at which the stock is automatically put up for sale. This strategy takes the emotion out of making critical trading decisions. When this type of order is entered, once your stock reaches the stop point, the order transforms into a market order.

Stop Order Buy

To get in on a stock rally at the exact point you want in, you can place a stop order to buy. Let's say Intel (INTC) is currently selling at $19 per share. If the price climbs to $22, you'd like to buy it because you think the price will continue to rise. Therefore, you put in a stop order to buy at $22. Once Intel hits $22 per share, your stop order automatically becomes a market order. Your order might be filled at your stop point of $22. However, since the stop order becomes a market order at your set stop point, you might also end up paying more or less for the stock. The price might rise to $22.50, for instance, before your order is filled. Conversely, the stock might hit $22 and then drop; you might end up buying it for $21.50.

Stop Order Sell

Let's say you bought that Intel stock at $22 per share. You can now place a stop order to sell if the stock price drops to $20. Once the stock hits your set stop point, called a hard stop, your stop order to sell becomes a market order. Again, that means your order might end up being filled at a higher or lower price, depending on the market price at the time your order is filled.

Another way to lock in profits is with a trailing stop, which sets the stop point as a percentage of the price as it's rising, then kicks in when the price falls. For example, a 10% trailing stop for a stock trading at $22 would be $2.20, so a sell order would kick in if the stock fell to $19.80. If the stock price rose, though, the sell point would rise with it. For example, if the price climbed to $30 per share, a fall down to $27 per share (a loss of 10%) would trigger a sale.

STOCKBROKERS

May I Take Your Order?

As an investor, you have multiple options for choosing a stockbroker. Before you make your selection, you need to evaluate your needs, comfort level, personal commitment, and available time for research, as well as your desire to be personally involved in your investment portfolio. Also be sure you are aware of any fees associated with your choice of broker and service level.

At the most basic level, a broker simply fills your orders and does nothing else, so that's all you pay for. As you move up in service levels from there, you'll notice fees and costs climbing as well. And while virtually every type of broker offers some form of online account access, which may include trades, that doesn't make them all online brokers.

DISCOUNT BROKERS

If you are ready, willing, and able to investigate potential companies on your own, then a discount broker may fit the bill. Many individuals find that taking charge of their investments is an empowering experience. Once they become acquainted with all of the available information, many investors feel like they are in the best position to handle their own investments, and are happy to be in the driver's seat.

Commissions charged by brokerage houses were deregulated in 1975, and this decision was truly the beginning of the ascent of the discount broker. Trades could be conducted for far less money than investors were used to paying at full-service brokerage firms. Discount brokers are now offering more services than ever before. Combine that with today's new and faster technology, and investors have all of the investment information they need right at their disposal.

Online-only brokers are available only on the Internet; there is no option to walk into a traditional broker's office and talk with someone face-to-face. Online brokers have expanded the range of services they offer over the Internet and now many provide services similar (sometimes superior) to those offered by full-service brokers in areas like research assistance and personalized trading advice.

With ever-accelerating developments on the Internet, the opportunity for self-education keeps improving. Beginning investors now have access to many of the same resources as full-service brokers. With this access to data, the demand for full-service brokers is diminishing. A little enthusiasm and determination on your part can pay off. With the wealth of online information, you can stay informed on everything from a company's new product rollouts to the ten most highly traded stocks on any given day. You can also get real-time quotes and in-depth analyses.

The proliferation of online discount brokers has made it possible to trade around the clock for a nominal fee—or even no fee at all. Trading online is ideal if you have done your homework and know exactly which stock you want to own.

FULL-SERVICE BROKERS

If you want someone else to do most of the legwork, you might opt for a full-service broker. Of course, full-service brokers charge a premium for their input. There is no guarantee that a full-service broker will steer you in the direction of massive capital gains. It is also true that many such brokers tend to pay more attention to their large accounts (clients investing more than $250,000, for example) than the smaller ones.

Know Who You're Trusting

If you want to work with a full-service broker, get a reference from someone you know and trust who has actually used her financial services. Don't rely on a referral from someone who knows the broker professionally, but who hasn't ever relied on her financial advice.

Some experts believe that if you have investments totaling more than $100,000, you may want to explore the possibility of at least consulting a full-service broker. If you decide to do that, find a broker who both shares your basic investment philosophy and gives you several investment options to choose from. Choose a broker with extensive investment experience and a track record trading in both bull and bear markets. Most important, make sure you feel comfortable with the broker personally, and that he is willing to listen to your input, and answer all your questions without hesitation.

It's perfectly acceptable (and advisable) to interview potential brokers. Ask how long they have been in this business and inquire about their formal education and investment philosophy. Find out if they rely only on their brokerage firm's reports when making stock recommendations. You can also ask more pointed questions, like how their clients fared during a recent downturn, or what strategies they use to protect their clients from losses. Also make sure the broker provides you upfront with a written list of fees you'll be charged, along with an explanation of when charges will be incurred. If the broker gives you the runaround or refuses to answer your questions, find someone else to work with.

MONITORING THE BROKERS

Becoming acquainted with the broker fee structure is crucial. In many cases, you may be charged for services you didn't know you were getting—and wouldn't use even if you knew you could. You also want to inquire about the fees associated with opening, maintaining, and closing an account; getting checks; participating in investment profiles; buying and selling securities; and attending various seminars. To circumvent potential discrepancies, it's important that you obtain this information in writing and in advance—and not after the fact.

The Financial Industry Regulatory Authority (FINRA) can answer your questions about the practices of a particular broker by looking up his past record regarding any disciplinary actions taken or complaints that have been registered against him. They can also confirm whether the broker is licensed to conduct business in your state.

Another Way to Protect Investors

FINRA (Financial Industry Regulatory Authority) was created in July 2007 when the National Association of Securities Dealers (NASD) merged with the regulation committee of the NYSE. Before that, NASD took the lead with consumer-broker issues. The NASD also had primary responsibility for the running of the NASDAQ exchange and other over-the-counter markets, as well as administering licensing exams for financial professionals.

In addition to being the primary nongovernmental agency dedicated to protecting the investing public, FINRA also regulates every securities firm that operates in the United States—nearly 3,400 firms. To get the job done, FINRA employs about 3,600 professionals in nineteen offices throughout the United States, with its main offices in New York City and Washington, DC.

PROTECT YOURSELF FROM DISHONEST BROKERS

The vast majority of stockbrokers operate with integrity, but there are also a lot of scammers out there who are looking to score profits at the expense of investors. The SEC and FINRA do their best to track down swindlers, but they can't catch them all. Your best defense against broker fraud is due diligence and personal references.

Even thorough background checks can't smoke out every scam artist, especially when it's so very easy for them to create realistic websites that mirror those of well-respected investment firms. So after you've done your homework, pay attention to what your broker does and how he treats you. The dishonest ones will use tricks to increase their commissions, urge you to buy sham investments, even funnel funds out of your account. If you know what to look for, though, you won't be caught with a drained brokerage account.

One nasty trick to look out for is called churning. Brokers who engage in churning make trades in your account purely for the sake of generating commissions. Churning especially benefits brokers who work on straight commission—the more trades they make, the more pay they take home. The impact on your portfolio can be devastating: Excessive commissions eat away at your funds while the value of your investments decreases. Any trade that has no reasonable purpose is a churn trade, even if it happens just once. If you notice trades in your account that don't make sense, contact your broker immediately, before it can happen again.

FINANCIAL PLANNERS

If you need all-around money management advice, consider hiring a professional financial planner. These people go beyond handling your investments—they aid you in matters relating to insurance, taxes, trusts, and real estate. The cost of doing business with a financial planner can vary considerably. If you opt for a financial planner, consider hiring a fee-based planner rather than a commission-based planner. If the planner works on commission alone, it may be in her best interest to encourage heavy trading. While some planners charge a flat hourly rate, others may charge a fee that is based on your total assets and trading activity. In this type of arrangement, you are responsible for paying the financial planner even if you do not follow any of her suggestions. Other planners operate with a combination of fee-based charges and commission. Here, you may pay less per trade, but you are also responsible for paying additional fees.

IPOS

The Ground Floor

Initial public offerings, or IPOs, mark the first time stock in a corporation is made available to the public; that's why IPOs are referred to as "going public." This undertaking helps small, young, privately owned companies obtain the financing they need to expand their businesses.

IPOs can be very complex and intricate. There are a lot of rules and regulations governing both the underwriters and the issuers. However, there are some basic steps all IPOs follow.

First, the company going public, now called the issuer, works with an underwriter to figure out all the details, which include what types of shares they will issue, how many, the best offering price, and the optimal timing.

Underwriters

An underwriter raises investment capital on behalf of the company that is issuing an IPO. Typically these underwriters are banks or large financial institutions.

Next, the preliminary registration documents are prepared and filed with the proper governing bodies, including the SEC. This paperwork contains crucial information about the offering and about the company along with filing details, which include things like current financial statements, information about key management personnel, how they plan to use the money they raise, and how much stock will be held by company insiders.

While the SEC confirms the information in those documents, a time frame called the "cooling off period," the underwriter creates a preliminary prospectus to generate interest in the offering.

When the SEC signs off on the offering, finalized documents and a final prospectus are submitted for approval. This set of papers includes the official offering date, known as the effective date, when the shares can finally be sold. That final prospectus is legally binding, and it includes the firm offering price for the IPO shares. This is the only time that a stock price is fixed. Once they hit the secondary market, stock prices are determined by investor sentiment—whatever amount someone is willing to pay.

IPO DEAL STRUCTURES

When underwriting an IPO, there are two main ways to structure the deal. Under the terms of a "best efforts" agreement, the underwriter sells the offering company's securities, but does not guarantee the amount of money that will be raised. A "firm commitment" structure, on the other hand, means that the underwriter has guaranteed that a specific amount of capital will be raised. They do that by buying the entire offering, then reselling it to public investors.

Most of the time, IPOs are underwritten by a group of investment banks; that group is called a syndicate. Operating with a group helps spread the risk of the IPO among underwriters, so no one company carries the full weight of the offering.

RED HERRINGS AND THE DOG AND PONY SHOW

When a company is ready to go public, but the SEC hasn't yet given them the green light, its owners and their underwriter still have a lot of work to do. They have to get enough high-level investors interested in the shares they're offering to fund their corporation.

That starts with a "red herring," the colorful name given to the preliminary prospectus. This document contains virtually all the information about the company and its upcoming IPO except for a few key pieces of information: the offering price and the effective date.

With their red herring in hand, the company bigwigs and the underwriter go on the road, meeting with potential investors in an attempt to get them excited about investing in the new corporation. This road show is called the "dog and pony show," and it's a very important part of the IPO process. Without enough enthusiasm and anticipation surrounding the offering, they may not be able to raise enough capital to fully fund their venture.

ADVANCED INVESTING TECHNIQUES

Don't Try This at Home

For investors who love the thrill of high risk and the potential of increased rewards, margin buying and short selling can fulfill those itches. These techniques are not suitable for conservative, risk-averse investors, or for investors who really can't afford to lose money. This is because when you employ these strategies, you cross the line from investing into gambling, and you can lose even more than your original investment.

MARGIN BUYING

In the world of stock trading, margin buying means borrowing money to purchase stocks. Sounds simple, but it can get complicated very quickly, especially if the market moves suddenly in an unexpected direction. Margin buying can amplify investment gains and losses, which makes it a valuable but highly risky strategy.

Margin buying requires that you have a brokerage account that holds your investments, or at least some of them. The brokerage firm can lend you money, with those investments as collateral, for what is called a margin loan. If the value of your collateral investments drops down far enough, you'll get the usually dreaded margin call from your broker, and you'll have to pony up more securities or cash to meet the minimum requirements.

SELLING SHORT

When most investors buy stocks, they're hoping share prices will rise over time. This strategy is called buying long. Short selling, a daring investment strategy, takes the exact opposite approach: Short sellers are betting that the share price of the stock they just sold will decline, hopefully far and fast.

On top of that, selling short means selling shares that you don't already own: You sell them first, then plan to buy them when the price drops. In the middle is your broker, who loans you the shares to sell, and whom you pay back with the shares you buy. When you place the original order, you must be explicit: You're legally required to identify a short sale trade when you place the order. When you short a stock, you also must use a margin account. That account must be worth 150% of the value of the securities you're shorting. That 150% includes the short position.

Be Aware

If a stock you've borrowed pays a dividend, you will have to pay that dividend to the broker who loaned you the stock.

The biggest risk of short selling doesn't exist for buying long. This is because by selling short you can lose more than your original investment. If the stock price rises, you will take a loss. In fact, the loss potential is unlimited because there's no cap on how high the share price could climb. Regardless of the new share price, you're required to pay back every share you borrowed. For example, if you sold short shares at $20 per share, but the price rises to $50 per share, you would lose $30 per share. If you had bought those shares normally, hoping that the price would rise, and the price dropped to zero, you would only be out your $20-per-share investment.

Why would anyone take that unlimited risk? Because with careful research and objective motivation, short selling can be a way to profit when a stock is losing ground.

SHORT STEPS

The flow of a short sale depends in part on how the specific stock actually performs. We'll start with an example of a successful short. For the example, we'll ignore margin interest and brokerage fees, both of which would eat into your profits (or magnify your losses) in a real trade.

First, you identify a stock, let's call it ABC Corp., and you think it will drop in price soon. Right now, ABC is trading at $10 per share.

Next, you place a short sale order for 100 shares of ABC, a total of $1,000, with your broker. Before he'll execute the deal, the broker makes sure you have at least $500 in your margin account (50% of $1,000).

Your broker borrows those 100 shares of ABC Corp., sells them on the open market, and puts the $1,000 proceeds into your account.

A few days later, the ABC share price drops to $9 per share. You buy 100 shares at that price, and return them to your broker, for a $100 profit.

But if the stock price instead climbed to $12 per share, the story would go differently. If you decided to wait rather than buy the stock at $12, you would have to add another $100 to your margin account (50% of the $200 price difference). Let's say the stock stuck at $12 per share, and you decide to buy it to close out your short position so as not to potentially lose even more money. As a result, your overall loss would be $200.

ANNUAL REPORTS

An Investment in Knowledge

Most people would rather walk over hot coals than peruse the endless rows of numbers found in financial documents. Corporations understand that, and so they fill their annual reports with glossy color photos and colorful commentary. Corporations also know that a lot of people assume that a heavy, glossy report means a successful year. The numbers inside, though, may tell a completely different story. It's up to you to get comfortable with the numbers. When you do, you'll be able to look past the glossy pictures and discover the truth about a company's successes and failures.

If you're already a shareholder, you'll automatically get a copy of the annual report every year. If you haven't yet invested in the company, you can simply call and ask for one or look at it online. Every company's report looks different, and they may be assembled in different orders. However, every publicly traded company's annual report contains the same basic items:

- Letter from the chairman of the board (expect a big pile of spin here)
- A description of the company's products and services (more spin)
- Financial statements (read the footnotes carefully; they contain some of the meat)
- Management discussion (sort of a big picture look at the company, with a little spin)
- CPA opinion letter (read this to make sure the company's financial position is accurately represented)
- Company information (locations, officer names, and contact information)

- Historical stock data (including dividend history and dividend reinvestment plan program information)

GETTING THROUGH THE GLOSS

Don't judge a company's success by the look of its annual report. Stuffed with gorgeous full-color photos on heavy glossy pages, these reports aim to show the corporation in the best possible light. By focusing on positive results (no matter how insignificant) and possible future plans, a company can redirect investors' eyes away from troubling events and disappointing numbers.

With its professional presentation, the annual report highlights letters from the CEO and chairman who put their spin on the company's prospects as they describe the business. They fill the report with graphs and charts that look positive, but these graphics may not really say much when you look a little deeper.

So while the gloss may be more interesting to read, it's important for you to look at the numbers too. After all, the numbers are of vital importance to investors, especially when it comes to the success or failure of the stocks they own or want to own.

FINANCIAL STATEMENTS

The financial statements in the annual report contain basically the same information as in the Form 10-K that the company filed with the SEC, but that information may be more abbreviated here. The three main statements you'll want to review are the:

1. Balance sheet
2. Income statement
3. Cash flow statement

The balance sheet gives you a snapshot of the corporation on the last day of the fiscal year. This report shows the company's assets, liabilities, and equity: what they own, what they owe, and their net worth. Assets are generally listed in order of liquidity, beginning with cash and ending with fixed assets (things like manufacturing plants and heavy equipment).

The income statement shows you the company's profitability over the year. It starts with revenues, then subtracts costs and expenses to get to the net profit or loss, the bottom line.

Profits Don't Mean Cash

Just because a company reports profits on its income statement doesn't mean that the company has cash. Profits and cash are not the same thing, and a company can have one without the other.

The third report all investors should review and understand is the cash flow statement. This report tracks how cash has moved in and out of the company during the year. Investors can use it to follow the cash trail. The report also tells you where the money came from, which is crucial information if you're considering buying the company's stock. Money that came from operations is what you want to see; it shows that the company is successfully selling its products and services and managing its costs and expenses. If the cash inflow instead comes from borrowing or issuing more stock, that could raise concerns about the profit potential of the company.

READ THE FOOTNOTES

There's a common saying among financial professionals: Accountants hide the problems in the footnotes. That's because financial statement footnotes are a lot like fine print: text that we all know we should read, but don't. The truth is, many (if not most) of us don't have the patience to get all the way through it. Corporations know that, and use it to their advantage.

That sounds shady, but it's not. In fact, it's perfectly legal. Moreover, it is extremely common for corporations to disclose important information in the footnotes to their financial statements. Even if a company has nothing to hide, these footnotes are where management can offer expanded insight into current operations and future plans—information investors need to know. While the financial statements contain all the numbers, the footnotes explain those numbers: how they were calculated, and where they came from, along with a deeper explanation of the results.

In the first section of footnotes, you'll usually find the details of the company's accounting practices, such as which valuation methods they've chosen to use and when they recognize revenue. These choices reveal critical aspects of the corporation's earnings. To judge whether their choices make sense, you can find out what the standard is for that industry, and whether this company is following that standard. If it isn't, and this company is using a more aggressive accounting method, then it could be a warning sign that the company is trying to obscure negative performance or is using bookkeeping tricks to make their performance seem better than it is.

Why Recognition Time Matters

When shopping online, you know that some companies charge your credit card as soon as you click the "place my order" button, while others wait until your item has been shipped. Revenue recognition timing follows a similar principle. Some companies account for revenue when a product is ordered, others when a product is delivered. The distinction makes a difference for how they measure sales. A company that changes from one method to another can greatly distort its revenue figures.

The next section of the footnotes usually spells out details and disclosures, information the company is required to provide that doesn't quite fit into the financial statements. Examples of information normally found here include details about:

- ESOPs (employee stock ownership plans)
- Outstanding stock options
- Long-term debt
- Ongoing or upcoming legal battles
- Error corrections
- Accounting adjustments
- Changes in accounting procedures

Keep in mind, like the fine print in credit card agreements, the language in financial statement footnotes can be full of legal jargon, making it even more difficult to wade through. Though it's not always the case, longer paragraphs and more challenging language are often used to hide what the corporation doesn't want the investors to read. For example, Enron disclosed a lot of their shenanigans in the footnotes of their financial statements, but virtually no one bothered to read them.

STOCK TABLES

All in a Row

Stock data offer critical current information about stock prices, usually presented in a table format. In order to monitor your stock investments accurately, it is vital that you become adept in understanding stock data. Stock table information may vary slightly among different publications and websites, but the basic information is generally presented in a similar manner.

There are a few things you should know about stock data. Online information will be current, while printed information will be based on the prior day. When you search online, you can look for the information on one stock at a time or on that day's market overview. Additionally, you will need to learn some stock terminology, including the following:

- **Previous close.** The closing price from the prior trading day.
- **Open.** The first price for a trade executed on the current day.
- **52-week range.** The highest and lowest prices for which the stock was traded over the past fifty-two weeks.
- **Company symbol.** The ticker symbol (the abbreviated name) of the corporation that issued the stock.
- **Volume.** How many shares have been traded that day.
- **P/E (price-to-earnings) ratio.** This number is calculated by dividing the share price by the corporation's earnings per share.

One thing that puzzles stock market newcomers: Why doesn't today's open match yesterday's close? The open and close both reflect the price people are willing to pay for a particular stock, and a lot can change between 4:00 p.m. one day and 9:30 a.m. the next. The twenty-four-hour news cycle combined with an upsurge in after-hours trading can cause differences between the two prices.

Most major Internet news sites post up-to-the-minute stock tables, and many of them are interactive so you can click through and see daily news information about a company or an industry. To get an instant quote for any company's stock, just type the ticker symbol into a search engine, and the most current information will appear. You should see the same basic data that appears in the full stock table, along with extra information, like market capitalization, three-month average volume, and historic pricing.

TICKER SYMBOLS

What's in a Nickname?

Stock or ticker symbols are the abbreviations used to represent a stock (and other types of investments like mutual funds and ETFs, or exchange-traded funds). The symbols are primarily used to help investors and traders keep track of and find information about a security. Whenever an investor uses a quoting service, he will need to enter in the ticker symbol in order to get the right data.

The company usually creates its own stock symbol, and the symbol typically represents the name of the corporation. For example, the ticker symbol for Microsoft is MSFT, and the ticker symbol for Archer Daniels Midland is ADM. However, not all symbols correlate directly with the name of the company they represent. For example, the stock symbol for Anheuser-Busch is BUD, and Harley-Davidson goes by HOG. It's important for investors to learn the correct symbol for each company they invest in and each company they're researching for potential investment; some symbols are quite similar, and it's critical to use the right one.

Ticker Trivia

Cedar Fair, LP, is a publicly traded company with the seemingly unlikely stock symbol FUN. But the symbol is more appropriate than you'd think. Cedar Fair owns eleven amusement parks around the United States. You may have been to Dorney Park (Pennsylvania), Kings Dominion (Virginia), or Knott's Berry Farm (California), all of which are owned by Cedar Fair.

EXTRA LETTERS

The number of letters in a company's ticker symbol lets you know on which exchange the stock trades. The NYSE uses stock symbols of up to three letters for their listed companies. Companies listed on the NASDAQ exchange use four letters if the stock issued is common stock.

Sometimes, though, you'll see extra letters added on to a ticker symbol, and that can happen for a lot of different reasons. While most often those extra letters indicate some kind of problem with the shares, sometimes they simply designate a different share type.

A designation of "PR" following the ticker symbol indicates preferred stock on the NYSE. That PR may also be followed by another letter to designate the class of shares. For example, the ticker symbol for Bank of America preferred stock Series L trades as BAC.PRL. Corporations that offer multiple classes of common stock also have an extra letter tacked on their ticker symbols. For example, the two classes of Berkshire Hathaway stock trade as BRK.A and BRK.B.

Sometimes NASDAQ stocks have similar extra letters, denoting share class or preferred status. Other times, it's because the security being traded is not a common stock. When a stock trading on the NASDAQ has a fifth letter added to its ticker symbol, it's time to pay close attention, especially if that letter is E or Q. Each fifth letter has a specific meaning. The fifth letter codes are explained in the accompanying table.

CODE	MEANING	CODE	MEANING
A	Class A	N	3rd Class Preferred Shares
B	Class B	O	2nd Class Preferred Shares
C	Issuer Qualifications Exceptions	P	1st Class Preferred Shares
D	New Issue	Q	Bankruptcy Proceedings
E	Delinquent in Filings with the SEC	R	Rights
F	Foreign	S	Shares of Beneficial Interest
G	1st Convertible Bond	T	With warrants or with rights
H	2nd Convertible Bond	U	Units
I	3rd Convertible Bond	V	When issued and when distributed
J	Voting	W	Warrants
K	Nonvoting	X	Mutual Fund
L	Miscellaneous situations	Y	American Depository Receipt (ADR)
M	4th Class Preferred Shares	Z	Miscellaneous situations

Shares traded over-the-counter (OTC) typically have five (sometimes four) letters.

CHANGING SYMBOLS

There are a few reasons a corporate ticker symbol might change. In some cases, the company initiates the change itself. Other times a symbol is altered by the exchange that the stock trades on, or it can be changed by a governing body like FINRA.

The two main reasons a company would change its own symbol are because of a name change or because it has merged with or been acquired by another company. In the case of a true merger, where a new company is formed, the two companies' ticker symbols will both change to reflect the new business. When a company is acquired, it may change its symbol to that of the acquiring company. For example, Walgreens originally traded as WAG—in fact, it used that symbol for almost ninety years. After it bought up Alliance Boots, merging with one of the largest European drugstore chains, the symbol changed to WBA.

When a company's ticker symbol is changed by an outside entity, it is usually an indication that something has gone wrong. For example, a company can be delisted, meaning it is no longer allowed to trade on one of the major exchanges. If that happens, it will trade only over the counter.

TICKER TAPE

This Has Nothing to Do with Parades

If you've ever watched a financial news show on TV and seen a line of cryptic letters and numbers scrolling across the bottom of the screen, you've seen what's known as the ticker tape. That information, properly decoded, helps investors and other market watchers stay on top of market trends and stock prices as they change throughout the trading day.

Originally recorded on tiny strips of paper, the ticker tape now appears in electronic format. But its function is still the same: to record every single transaction that takes place on the floor of the exchange. Ticker tape was first created in 1867, thanks to the introduction of telegraph machines. The latest price figures were delivered by runners who brought the tape from the market floor to the traders' offices. With this system, the brokerage houses closest to the trading floor got the news first, a distinct advantage.

By the 1960s, the tapes moved faster, but there was still a lag between the time the trade occurred and the time it was recorded. That delay was sometimes as long as twenty minutes, veritable centuries in today's world of instantaneous trading.

Ticker Trivia

A tick refers to any movement in the price of a security. Whether it goes up or down, whether the change is minuscule or notable, every move counts as a tick.

Finally, in the mid-1990s, a real-time ticker changed the pace of information. Electronically captured and broadcast, the data was put in everyone's hands at the same time, so the physical tape is no longer needed.

The ticker appearing on the bottom of the TV screen reports the trades of a single stock exchange. Some channels or programs will scroll two tickers across the screen to supply information from two exchanges, most commonly the NYSE and NASDAQ.

DECODING THE TICKER

The swiftly scrolling ticker tape seems puzzling at first glance. Once you know how to decode it, though, you will discover that it offers a wealth of up-to-the-minute information.

To break down a ticker tape, let's look at a bit of the strip:

TICKER SYMBOL	SHARES TRADED	PRICE TRADED	CHANGE DIRECTION	CHANGE AMOUNT
TGT	3,786,702	111.07	Δ	1.55

First up is the ticker symbol, which identifies the company, in this case Target (TGT).

Next is shares traded, which refers to the size of the trade being quoted, in this case 3.8 million.

Price traded indicates the closing price for the stock.

The fourth bit of information, change direction, lets you know whether the stock price rose or fell compared to the closing price on the previous trading day. Change amount lets you know how much the current price differed from the closing price on the previous trading day. In our example, it means the price of a share of TGT is trading for $1.55 more than it did at the prior day's close.

Some tickers use different colors to let viewers see immediately which way a stock price is moving. Though there's some variation, most use green to show stocks trading higher, red to indicate stocks trading lower, and white to show stocks that haven't changed from the closing price on the previous trading day.

WHICH STOCKS MAKE THE TICKER?

With thousands of stocks and millions of shares trading every day, the ticker that rolls across the TV screen can't possibly include every single transaction. Only select quotes are displayed, and those are selected based on a few criteria: trading volume, how widely shares are held, price change, and breaking news. To get a spot on the ticker, a stock generally must be a big name or big news, and placement on the ticker varies minute to minute during trading hours. Stocks with high trading volume will show up more times than stocks with less trading volume, for example, and a company that's all over the news will get more play than a quietly trading corporation.

Once the exchanges have closed for the day, the ticker runs in alphabetical order and displays only the last quote of the day. The action resumes when the markets reopen the next morning.

INVESTOR MATH BASICS

Yes, You Have to Do Some Math

After you've narrowed your focus of potential stock purchases to a handful of companies, you should continue your research efforts by reviewing a few factors for each company. Find out about each company's earnings per share, price-to-earnings ratio, book value, price volatility, dividends, number of shares outstanding, and total return. These factors will give you greater insight into the stocks.

While some of the numbers (like earnings per share) can be pulled straight from a corporation's annual report, others may require a little math on your part (like price-to-book value ratio). Don't let the math stop you—it's all pretty straightforward and not terribly time-consuming. And the information you'll get from it is well worth the effort.

BOOK VALUE

Book value (which is also known as accounting value) shows a company's net worth, its equity. In a nutshell, book value tells you how much of the company is owned rather than owed. To calculate a company's book value per share, first subtract its total liabilities from its total assets (both of which you'll find on the balance sheet), and then divide that result by the number of shares of common stock outstanding.

Knowing this ratio can help you figure out whether the share price (the market value) makes sense as compared with the company's actual intrinsic value. Many experts say that a good way to find value stocks is to look for companies whose stock price is less than double their book value per share.

Visiting the Website

Corporate websites are an invaluable source of information in helping you make your investment decisions. Most have a separate section for investors that includes everything from a corporate overview to annual reports to SEC filings.

PROFIT MARGIN

When it comes to corporate profits, one of the most important pieces of information is the profit margin. This tells you what percentage of sales actually ends up as earnings. A company can have record-breaking revenues and meet every sales goal, but if it can't keep any of its earnings, what does that matter?

A company's profit margin is calculated by dividing its net income by its revenue. Generally speaking, higher profit margins are better, but like so many other factors, this one is relative. Looking at a single period's profit margin gives you a little information, but comparing it with other periods lets you see a pattern. For example, if a company has shown profit margins of 10% over the last five years except for one quarter where it shrank to 3%, that says something different than an average 10% profit margin that bounces around between 3% and 20% over the same period. The first example indicates steady, reliable profitability, which is a very desirable quality for a potential investment. The second example shows volatile and unpredictable profits, which don't bode well for the company's financial security. A pattern of consistently decreasing profit margin should throw up a red flag as this could indicate that the company is saddled with rising costs or is losing market share. In addition, it's helpful to compare the company's profit margin with its industry average. If it seems way out of whack, savvy investors will find out why.

PRICE VOLATILITY

Price volatility refers to how much the share price varies. It is usually calculated by looking at the difference between a stock's high and low prices over a set time period. This factor is important in determining the risk of a potential investment. You might not be as willing to pay a lot for a stock if you knew that its price had jumped up and down dramatically over the past few months.

In stocks, the term that describes price volatility is "beta." This is a quantitative measure of the variability when compared with the market as a whole. In most analysis, beta compares the changes in a stock's price against changes in the S&P 500 stock index. For example, a stock with a beta of 2 varies twice as much as the S&P 500. That stock can then be expected to rise in price by 40% if the S&P 500 rises by 20% or drop by 40% if the S&P 500 falls by 20%.

PAR, BOOK, AND MARKET VALUE

Three Numbers, Three Theories

There are a lot of numbers thrown around when people are talking about stocks. Some of those numbers matter a great deal, and some don't matter as much, at least not to investors. Among them are three different values: par, book, and market. Some people use these terms interchangeably, but they mean very different things.

PAR VALUE

The dollar amount actually listed on a stock's certificate is called par value. On common stock, this is usually a very small number, sometimes just a fraction of a cent. In fact, some stocks are issued with no par value. That's because par value is also redemption value, and a stockholder could redeem his shares for par value. For example, if par value was ten cents per share, and you had 10,000 shares of stock, you could legally redeem them for $1,000. If the company was floundering, and the market price actually dropped below the par value, the company would be on the hook if shareholders chose to redeem their stock (at least in theory). That's why it's very common for corporations to issue no-par common stock. Whether a corporation is allowed to issue no-par shares depends on the laws of its home state (where it was created rather than its base of operations).

While par value matters a lot from an accounting perspective, it doesn't have anything at all to do with stock price.

BOOK VALUE PER SHARE

In its most basic sense, the book value per share is the amount of money that would be doled out for each share of stock if a corporation had to fold. The calculation is based on the company's total equity, which works just like the equity in your home. To figure that out, you would take the value of your house and subtract the amount you owe on your mortgage. The result is the equity you have in your home, the amount of your house that you actually own.

It's the same for a corporation. To figure out the total equity, start with everything the company owns (its assets), then subtract everything the company owes (its liabilities). To figure out the book value per share, you take that total equity and divide it by the total number of common shares outstanding.

Sometimes, the calculation is not that straightforward. If the corporation has also issued preferred stock, for example, that claim would take priority over common stock shares, and would have to be added into the equation.

Book value per share is really a measure of the company's worth based on its balance sheet, which is a key financial statement that acts like a snapshot of the corporation at a specific moment in time.

MARKET VALUE

To an investor, market value is the most important of these three values because it reflects how the overall stock market feels about this company. It is literally the price you have to pay to buy shares.

While both earnings and earnings growth may be the most customary measures on which stock prices are based, several other factors come into play. Name recognition, for example, has a large impact on stock price because well-established household brands add value to a corporation simply through their existence. Well-respected and recognizable employees also can lead to increases in a company's stock price, as their inclusion gives investors confidence in the ongoing success of the corporation. Competitive barriers affect stock price as well because they can hinder other companies from entering an industry. For example, exclusive contracts can give a company a distinct edge, and keep competitors from poaching locked-in customers or suppliers.

The total market value of a corporation can change rapidly. You calculate this by multiplying the current stock market price by the total number of shares outstanding. If Corporation ABC has 10 million shares outstanding, and the current stock price is $25, then the total market value of the company would be $250 million. When brokers or analysts are talking about the value of a corporation, this is what they mean.

EARNINGS PER SHARE

The Real Bottom Line

Earnings are the whole point of business, and every company aims to improve its bottom line. Without sustained positive earnings, a corporation cannot survive. As a potential stockholder and part owner of a corporation, earnings are a crucial component to consider. In fact, for most investors, earnings is the number one criteria by which to judge a company.

Earnings per share, usually abbreviated as *EPS*, lets you know how much of the company's total earnings (also called profits or net income) is earmarked for each individual share of the corporation's stock. The math to calculate EPS is pretty straightforward: It's the company's reported net income divided by the number of common shares outstanding.

How Many Shares Are Out There?

The number of common shares outstanding is not set in stone. That's because there are a number of different ways to arrive at that number. The number of shares could be based simply on how many shares of common stock are actually outstanding on the last day of the period. Alternately, it could be calculated as the weighted average number of shares that have been outstanding during the period, which could be different if shares were either issued or bought back by the corporation. Finally, the number could represent what's known as diluted shares, which is a much more complicated calculation that takes into account how many shares would be outstanding if every security that could be converted into common stock (such as stock options and convertible preferred shares) were converted.

To fully evaluate EPS and growth, though, it's important to know how the corporation has calculated its earnings, and whether their computation methodology has changed over time. Generally speaking, corporations have a lot of leeway when it comes to figuring their earnings, and it's to their advantage to show earnings in the best possible light to keep investors focused on what the company wants them to see.

WHAT "EARNINGS" REALLY MEANS

At the basic level, earnings are calculated by subtracting a company's costs and expenses from their revenues (sales). When a company uses its resources (assets) effectively and efficiently, those revenues will be higher than the costs and expenses. As a result, the company will have positive earnings. When the opposite holds true, and costs exceed revenues, the company suffers a loss, or negative earnings.

Calculating earnings can be a complex proposition, and sometimes even a convoluted one. In fact, by applying different tax and accounting principles, the same underlying numbers can result in different reported earnings.

HOW CORPORATIONS MANIPULATE EARNINGS

Depending on a corporation's end game, they can color their earnings any way they want, as long as it's legal—and you'd be surprised by how many seemingly shady accounting practices are perfectly legal as long as they're disclosed. With all that flexibility, a company can easily manipulate their earnings number, and even report a different number to the media than they do to the SEC or the IRS. Because of this, investors need to know exactly what they're looking at, and how the corporation came up with the numbers.

SEC filings, including the Form 10-Q and the Form 10-K, are expected to follow a set of strict standards known as GAAP (generally accepted accounting principles). Even within these rules, though, there's a degree of flexibility that allows companies to make reporting choices, and those choices can greatly affect the bottom line.

Mind the GAAP

GAAP, which stands for "generally accepted accounting principles," is a set of clear-cut rules and procedures that corporations are expected to use to put together their financial statements. These principles are designed to help investors better use and understand a company's financial position by calling for consistency and fairness in reporting.

In addition to manipulating the numbers themselves, corporations may also employ some sleight of hand when it comes to announcing their earnings, especially if they haven't hit analyst projections and expectations. For example, a company could announce their earnings after the market closes on a Friday afternoon—a practice referred to as "burying the report"—so that investors can't act immediately on an unfavorable earnings report and potentially force the stock price down. Another way that corporations hide numbers is to release them as a downplayed afterthought, following more positive highlighted information. For example, a corporation might slip a poor earnings number into a statement that's primarily focused on an upcoming development (like a new product launch).

Though corporations are required to disclose all of the pertinent information related to earnings, they don't have to make it easy for you to find. Often, the information they don't want investors to see or focus on appears only in the footnotes to the financial statements.

EARNINGS GROWTH

Once you've got a handle on EPS, you can determine a company's growth rate by looking at how its earnings per share have changed over the years. When you're looking to buy stock in a corporation, finding one with a pattern of strong, consistent earnings growth makes a lot of sense. You can see if the stock you're interested in fits the bill by analyzing the company's earnings per share results over the past several years. This analysis will let you see how and which way these results may have changed, and whether any growth is expected to continue.

In addition to the rate of change, you'll want to consider the pace of change. Slow but consistent growth can be indicative of a stable company in a low-growth industry. Fast and fluctuating change may indicate great future growth potential, or it could mean the spike in earnings was temporary or due to a single factor that may not be repeatable.

PRICE-TO-EARNINGS (P/E) RATIO

You Paid How Much for That?!

One of the most basic and often-used measures of a stock's value is the price-to-earnings ratio, or P/E ratio. Though the calculation itself is simple and straightforward, dividing the per-share stock price by the current earnings per share (EPS), this key piece of data provides a wealth of information. Most important, it tells you how much you'll be paying for one dollar of the corporation's current earnings. While it might seem like looking for the lowest P/E ratios would be the best move for investors, that's far from the case. On top of that, what's considered "low" is relative.

Reviewing a company's price-to-earnings (P/E) ratio is an integral part of any stock selection process. Since stock prices reflect investor demand, this ratio tells you the price investors are currently willing to pay in proportion to the company's earnings. For example, a P/E ratio of 20 means that investors are willing to pay twenty times more for a stock than that stock's related earnings per share. That information is important, but it's just the starting point.

For one thing, many different stocks can have the same P/E ratio despite vast differences in stock price and earnings. For instance, a stock that's trading for $30 per share and posts $1.50 earnings per share would have a P/E ratio of 20; but so would a stock that's trading for $60 with earnings of $3 per share, or a stock trading at $5 per share with earnings of $0.25 per share.

Once you know the P/E ratio of a particular stock, you can look at the relationship of that stock's P/E ratio to others in the same class. In most instances, you can find a company's P/E ratio, and those of its peers, online (or in the newspaper). By comparing it with companies in the same category (for example, other mid-cap growth stocks) and in the same industry (for example, other technology companies), you can see how a particular corporation stacks up.

Where to Find Sector Ratios

Yahoo! Finance (www.finance.yahoo.com/sectors) provides sector P/E ratios in an easy-to-view format, and you can click any sector to see the P/E ratios for industries in that sector. Using that information, you can quickly see how a company you're interested in fares in comparison to similar companies in the same industry.

When you're investigating a particular stock, compare its P/E ratio with P/E ratios of other companies in the same industry and for that industry as a whole. Since every industry has its own unique qualities, you will want to find out what the average P/E is for that particular sector. If a company has an exceptionally high or low P/E compared to others in its industry, it's not necessarily a bad thing, but it is important to find out the reason why their ratio is off. For example, a low P/E ratio could indicate that the company's growth has been stagnant, that the company is burdened with excessive debt, or that the stock could simply be undervalued—making it a great buy for value investors. A company with a relatively high P/E ratio could be overpriced, or it could have dependable future earnings growth brought on by a recent expansion, acquisition, or new product line—making it a good choice for growth investors.

INDUSTRY AND SECTOR RATIOS VARY WIDELY

Context is crucial when you're evaluating stocks, and delving into P/E ratios is no different: They need to be seen in the context of their business peers.

Some industries have consistently lower P/E ratios than others. For example, classic industries that have been around for decades, even centuries, tend to have lower P/E ratios than new or up-and-coming industries. Stocks of utility companies, for example, virtually always come with much lower P/E ratios than technology stocks do.

It's also important to see how a company (or an industry) stacks up against the broader sector it belongs to. That information helps you determine whether a company might be an industry leader or laggard.

P/E ratios can vary widely from sector to sector, and even within a sector or industry. But this additional knowledge adds to the full picture of the stock you're evaluating.

THE PEG RATIO

Back to the Future

Earnings per share (EPS) and the price-to-earnings (P/E) ratio measure what's happened in the corporation's past. That's important information to be sure, but as an investor, you care even more about what will happen next. The PEG ratio, or price-to-earnings growth ratio, gives interested investors a glimpse into a company's potential for growth.

Let's start with how the PEG is calculated: Divide the P/E ratio by the annual EPS growth rate. This gives you an indication of the market's expectations of the company's future earnings. Like the P/E ratio, lower PEG ratios can indicate undervalued stock. Taken together with the P/E ratio, it gives a more complete picture of the stock's true value, and whether it deserves a place in your portfolio.

You can use the PEG to help compare stocks with different price and earnings pictures to see which makes more sense for your investment strategy. Let's say ABC Corp., an up-and-coming biotech company, has a P/E ratio of 200 and an earnings growth rate of 40%. Another stock you're intrigued by, XYZ Company, an established soda manufacturer, has a P/E ratio of 40 and a 10% earnings growth rate. While that 40% growth rate makes ABC Corp. look like the obvious winner, calculating the PEG may tell a different story. The PEG for ABC works out to 5 (200 ÷ 40). The PEG of XYZ works out to 4 (40 ÷ 10). Based on those results, the tried-and-true soda company has a better PEG ratio as compared to the biotech firm, because investors are paying less for expected future growth.

TOTAL RETURNS

Show Me the Money!

The calculations we looked at earlier are all used for investment selection. Total returns looks at a different side of investing: how well your stocks are performing for you.

Most investors in stocks tend to think about their gains and losses only in terms of share price changes. But savvy investors also think about another very important part of the picture: dividends. Although dividend yields may seem more important when you are looking for income, and price changes dominate the scene when you buy growth stocks, your total return on any stock investment is extremely important. Knowing a stock's total return indeed makes it possible for you to compare your investment with other stock investments, but it also makes it much easier for you to see how your stock measures up to other types of holdings, such as corporate bonds, treasuries, and mutual funds.

To figure out the total returns on a stock you own, first add the change in the stock price (or subtract it if the price has gone down) since the beginning of the year to the dividends you've earned over the past twelve months. Then divide that sum by the stock price at the beginning of the twelve-month period. For example, suppose you buy a stock at $45 per share and receive $1.50 in dividends for the next twelve-month period. At the end of the period, let's say that the stock is selling for $48 per share. Your calculations would look like this:

- Dividend: $1.50
- Price change: up $3.00 per share

- $1.50 + $3.00 per share = $4.50
- $4.50 ÷ $45.00 = 0.10

Your total return is a 10% increase.

But suppose, instead, that the price had dropped to $44 per share by the end of the period. Then your calculation would look like this:

- Dividend: $1.50
- Price change: down $1.00 per share
- $1.50 – $1.00 per share = $0.50
- $0.50 ÷ $45.00 = 0.011

Your total return is only a 1.1% increase.

Knowing your total returns on an investment will help you decide if that stock still deserves a place in your portfolio, but it's not the only number to consider. Looked at together with other factors, like earnings growth, and measured against the appropriate benchmark index, you can get a more complete picture of the security's real value.

FIVE CHARACTERISTICS OF GREAT COMPANIES

Kick the Tires, Check the Teeth

A lot of stock analysis focuses on numbers, most of them representing information from the past. But since buying stock represents investing in the future, it's important to get a real feel for a company's prospects by considering the following five traits:

- **Sound business model.** You want to single out a company that has a solid business plan and a good grasp of where it wants to be in the years ahead, and a plan to get there. A company with a clear focus has a better chance of reaching its goals and succeeding than a company that just rolls along without a concrete plan.
- **Superior management.** An experienced, innovative, and progressive management team has the best chance of leading a company into the future. Star managers have had a major impact on their prospective companies, and a company will often witness dramatic changes when a new management team comes on board. When key management leaves an organization, you will often see major changes in the way a company operates.
- **Significant market share.** When a majority of individuals rely upon the products and/or services of a designated company, odds are the company has good insight into consumer preferences. Industry market leaders usually have a well-thought-out vision. However, the company with the strongest performance doesn't always translate into the best stock to buy. Be careful and look more closely at markets that have a glut of competitors;

sometimes the second-best company makes the best stock investment.

- **Competitive advantages.** A company that is ahead of the pack will often be on top of cutting-edge trends and industry changes in areas like marketing and technology. You want to single out those companies that are—and are likely to stay—one step ahead of the competition.
- **New developments.** If a company places a high priority on research and development, it's likely to roll out successful introductions. If the product or service takes off, the stock price may very well follow.

THE BUFFETT APPROACH TO SUCCESS

Many individuals want to emulate the successful investors. And why not? Warren Buffett, for example, has earned his fame by investing in quality companies instead of relying on technical analysis strategies. Buffett believes that if you buy stock in quality companies, you have no reason to sell your investments unless there is a serious underlying problem behind a price dip. Buffett believes that investors should understand a company and its industry before making any investment decisions.

Ticker Trivia

One of Warren Buffett's most famous quotes sums up his strategy in a nutshell: "Rule No. 1: Never lose money. Rule No. 2: Never forget Rule No 1."

Although Buffett prefers to buy companies at prices below their potential, price is not the sole consideration in his stock selection process. Buying quality companies for the long haul is key. If one of your star companies suffers a dip in its stock price, Buffett says, it might be a good chance to pick up some additional shares.

INVESTOR PSYCHOLOGY

Taking Emotion Out of the Deal

It turns out that many individual investors often act irrationally when it comes to making their buy and sell decisions. For example, they might trade based on the popularity of a stock rather than its value or growth potential. This emotional trading usually leads to losses, yet these investors continue to make the same types of investment decisions. The relatively new field of behavioral finance examines these poor decision-making strategies and links them to market irregularities like crashes and bubbles.

Here's how behavioral finance tends to work: People jump to buy a stock because it's hot. That drives up the price, and more investors snap up shares. It makes no difference that the company has an unproven track record or is loaded with debt—all that matters in the heat of the trading moment is the excitement of owning this very popular stock. The number of investors who jump on that bandwagon alters the patterns and directions of the stock market—and not necessarily for the better.

The irony is that while many investors have no problem plowing their hard-earned money into portfolios stuffed with complicated creatures like biotech or nanotechnology stocks, these very same investors pause when given the opportunity to invest in a classic alternative investment like a hedge fund or a real estate trust.

AVOID THE HERD MENTALITY

When people first start investing, they often believe they'll make their investment decisions based purely on facts and research. But despite these good intentions they end up letting their emotions run the show. This can lead to investments that don't fit into the investor's plans and portfolios. For example, it's very tempting to follow the herd and buy what everyone else is buying. But when a bubble bursts, like the tech bubble did at the end of the 1990s, investors learned the hard way not to invest in a sector just because everyone else is doing it.

Ticker Trivia

You can't outperform the market if you buy the market. Bernard Baruch, an economic advisor to Woodrow Wilson and Franklin Roosevelt, was a firm believer in this principle of market investing, saying repeatedly, "Never follow the crowd." If you buy with the crowd, you will achieve the same results as everyone else, good or bad.

Following the crowd is a major part of behavioral finance, and many investment professionals now use the lessons learned from this area of study to inform their overall strategies. Traditional market analysis is founded on the idea that investors behave rationally and make their decisions only after carefully considering all available information. Behavioral finance adds a more human component to understanding the actions of investors by applying some basic principles of psychology.

KNOW YOURSELF

Understanding yourself is an integral component to mapping out an investment plan. What's right for you might be disastrous for another investor. Knowing your long-term goals and determining how much risk you can tolerate is critical when dealing with stocks because of their inherent volatility. Look back at your investor profile and let it guide you.

If you find at any point after you've invested that you simply cannot handle the market's mood swings, you may want to reevaluate your strategy. Even though your investment plan is not set in stone, you should be fully aware of your reasons for changing your original strategy. Maintaining realistic expectations will keep beginning investors from growing frustrated, disappointed, and disillusioned. It's unrealistic to expect a 15% return on your investment if you aren't willing to take any risks. Understanding market volatility and your reactions to it can help you create the best portfolio.

Once you have developed a strategy you're comfortable with, don't second-guess yourself. Stick with the plan until it makes sense to reassess; don't let herd movements derail your strategy. No matter what your investing style, you have a good shot at success if you invest in high-quality companies you believe will—among other things—continue a track record of good financial execution and financial management.

BARONS, TITANS, AND TYCOONS

How Unbridled Greed Built America

The roots of today's big traders go all the way back to the beginnings of the US stock market, a time when investing resembled the Wild West and investors acted like gamblers more often than not. It was a time when great names were being made, names that still resonate today: Morgan, Carnegie, Rockefeller, Vanderbilt.

Among these big traders, billions of dollars were earned and lost. Some of these men came from money, others from poverty. Their insights and foresights helped paved the way for modern industry and trans-American transportation. Many of them had run-ins with the law, others with criminals, and several faced off against each other. Through their riveting tales, we can begin to see how the financial markets shaped the United States, and how these men shaped the markets.

J.P. MORGAN

Though today we think of J.P. Morgan as an investment bank, John Pierpont Morgan was one of the most famous tycoons ever to trade on Wall Street. Morgan invested in dozens of enterprises, from railroads to steel mills to Edison's electric company.

Born with a silver spoon in his mouth, Pierpont (as he liked to be called) began his financial career courtesy of his vastly wealthy father, a leader in the banking industry. And while his father arranged his first job with a solid New York bank, Morgan soon stood out as a brilliant—and ruthless—financial mind.

Having started in banking, Morgan truly understood investing. He used his knowledge, skill, and experience to take over the US financial markets. When the Panic of 1873 hit the US economy, Morgan didn't flinch; he emerged even richer, with his position in the world of finance solidified. His most famous investment was buying Carnegie Steel for $480 million in 1901. With that, Morgan created US Steel, and his investment more than doubled in size within just ten years.

Despite tangles with antitrust laws, congressional investigations, and his reputation as a callous robber baron, Morgan twice bailed out the US government during financial panics. In fact, during the Panic of 1907, Morgan pledged his money (and convinced others to join him) to stabilize the US banking system.

ANDREW CARNEGIE

Born to working class parents in Dunfermline, Scotland, Andrew Carnegie had none of the childhood advantages that blessed J.P. Morgan. But by the end of his life, Carnegie's wealth rivaled Morgan's. In fact, the two fortunes collided when Carnegie sold his flagship steel company to Morgan.

As he began his teenage years, Carnegie's family made the exhausting journey to the United States, settling in the small town of Allegheny, Pennsylvania. There, Andrew Carnegie got his first job, earning little more than one dollar a week in a cotton mill. But Carnegie's natural intelligence and motivation were quickly recognized, and he was soon promoted to office work. In this career, he caught the attention of a Pennsylvania Railroad executive, Thomas Scott, who hired Carnegie to be his personal secretary.

Under Scott's employ, Carnegie saved his money. And then he began to invest it. In fact, Scott told Carnegie about an upcoming sale of shares in a business called the Adams Express Company. Though he needed his mother, Margaret, to mortgage their family home to come up with the full $500 needed to buy ten shares, Carnegie made that very first investment, which began to pay off quickly with handsome dividends. Carnegie relished receiving dividends, earning money without toiling, and he quickly reinvested them to earn even more. As it turned out, Carnegie had an incredible talent for peering into the future and investing in what he saw ahead.

While he was fully enmeshed in the business of the railroad, Andrew Carnegie became interested in other types of companies. For example, along with idea man Theodore Woodruff, Carnegie was instrumental in bringing the first sleeper cars to the railroad. By the time he was thirty years old, Carnegie held investments in several industries, including ironworks and oil wells. He got involved with the Keystone Bridge Company, working to transform old wooden bridges into heavy-duty iron ones. And through all of these investments, Carnegie built himself an income that topped $50,000 a year, an astonishing feat during the Civil War era.

During that time, an Englishman named Henry Bessemer developed a process to transform large amounts of iron into steel. Whereas iron was tough but brittle, steel was durable and flexible, which made it easier to work with. When Andrew Carnegie learned of the Bessemer process, he poured money into the fledgling steel business, and he invested in a steel manufacturing plant right outside Pittsburgh. Carnegie expanded his holdings, and he built innovative new mills that would give him an enormous edge over his competitors. And by 1873, when the US economy slumped, Carnegie bought his competitors' mills, modernized them, and continued to rake in profits.

One key secret to Carnegie's vast financial success was an idea called vertical combination (sometimes called vertical integration). For example, he bought majority shares in the iron mines necessary to steel manufacturing, as well as shares in the railroads needed to move his products. These stepping stones come together to form a full path, increasing overall efficiency and reducing costs for the core business.

JOHN D. ROCKEFELLER

Known as the richest man in the world, John D. Rockefeller was notorious for his cutthroat business strategies, which included crushing his competition, then buying up all their assets.

Rockefeller was born to a poor family in Richford, New York. After dabbling in several industries, his interests turned to oil, and it was there that Rockefeller made his mark. Rockefeller turned the burgeoning oil industry on its head, profiting in ways no one had ever considered before, fueled by the big demand for kerosene (light bulbs had not yet been invented).

Kerosene comes from crude oil, converted during a largely wasteful refining process. Where everyone else in the industry saw waste, though, Rockefeller saw opportunity. He turned several crude oil by-products into moneymakers: selling petroleum jelly to medical companies, offering paraffin to candlemakers, and even creating a market for other waste by calling it "paving materials."

All of these products, including the premium kerosene, needed to be moved throughout the country. In those days, shipping was done primarily by rail. And with railroads competing for his extensive business, Rockefeller was able to insist on discounted rates in the form of rebates. With those steep savings, he was able to greatly undercut his competition, offer reduced prices to his customers, and crush his competitors.

During that time, in 1870, at age thirty, Rockefeller founded his crowning achievement, Standard Oil. He quickly bought up other oil retailers, turning Standard Oil into a corporation of corporations until it was broken up by the government into thirty-four separate companies, some of which can be traced to companies still operating today.

And when demand for kerosene dropped off, replaced with calls for gasoline as the new automobile industry got underway, Rockefeller quickly adapted his refineries to produce the new fuel, never missing a beat.

Ticker Trivia

John D. Rockefeller was the world's first billionaire, having earned more wealth than any other American in history.

CORNELIUS VANDERBILT

Born into poverty just before the turn of the century in 1794, Cornelius Vanderbilt later would come to the markets with a vengeance, ruthlessly taking over companies and industries by employing strategies never before seen (though now they're old hat). Branded a robber baron, Vanderbilt monopolized two industries crucial to the fledgling American economy: ships and railroads.

His story begins during a time when the country was going through seismic changes, and new technologies were rapidly making their way to the forefront of the economy; it was the time of an industrial revolution. Vanderbilt had an uncanny knack for understanding which new industries had the most potential. And when he identified one, he jumped straight in.

When he was just eleven years old, in 1805, Vanderbilt dropped out of school to go work for his father, an uneducated ferry operator. Just a few years later, he took $100 and bought a sailboat, which he used to shuttle goods and people between Manhattan and his home borough of Staten Island, recouping his initial investment in under a year. To keep his business afloat, young Vanderbilt began employing business tactics that would later become his hallmark: He offered often better service for a fraction of the price his rivals were charging. Before long, those competitors were forced to pay him to move, or go out of business themselves. Those moves seem obvious now, but before Vanderbilt, undercutting the competition was virtually unheard of.

Soon steamboats came along, and before the invention was a decade old, "Commodore" Vanderbilt learned how to pilot one. By the 1840s, he commanded more than 100 of the vessels, all known for their comfort, speed, and cheap prices.

Around that same time, Vanderbilt realized that railroads were the future of industry, and he plunked his money down as one of the first investors in railroad shares. But without the benefit of a transcontinental railroad—it hadn't yet been built—the shrewd entrepreneur shifted his attention to his shipping holdings, earning his first million. In 1864, having earned $30 million, seventy-year-old Vanderbilt bowed out of the shipping industry and returned his eagle eye focus to the railroads.

To outsiders, it may have seemed like he was just buying up stock in railroads. And he accumulated many, including the New

York Central, Canada Southern, Michigan Central, and Michigan Southern (among others). But Vanderbilt had a visionary plan: He intended to connect a route from New York all the way through to Chicago. Then he could put his standard strategy into play, which was to provide excellent service at very low prices to drown out any competition, and then form a monopoly.

Vanderbilt's plan hit a snag when he faced steep competition for the Erie Railroad. As he quietly bought up shares in the railroad, hoping to corner the market unnoticed, longtime competitor and business foe Daniel Drew set out to derail him.

From his inauspicious beginnings, Vanderbilt changed the direction of his life and became a self-made millionaire, leaving an estate worth an estimated $105 million when he died in 1877.

FAMOUS AND INFAMOUS INVESTORS

Whatever It Takes to Win

Over the span of centuries, the fortunes of the greatest investors have fascinated us, but their personal stories are often even more intriguing. Although these famed investors amassed great fortunes in the stock market, not all of them were able to hold onto that wealth.

From quirky misers to investing innovators, these men and women changed the shape of the stock market and the face of investing. Among these legends are millionaires, billionaires, and paupers. There was one man who nearly destroyed the Bank of England, and a wealthy woman known as the Witch of Wall Street. Each of these legendary investors greatly influenced the stock market we know today.

WARREN BUFFETT

$118 billion. That's the estimated net worth of legendary investor Warren Buffett as of November 2023. And the lion's share of that immense wealth comes from his shares in Berkshire Hathaway, a company he took over in 1962; a company that started out as a mere textile manufacturer. That company has morphed into a multinational conglomerate, with extensive holdings in many disparate industries: from banking to food to private aviation.

Buffett made his first investment when he was just eleven years old, six shares of a company called Cities Service Preferred (he gave three of those shares to his sister). That he chose to put his money in the market is not so surprising, considering his father was a stockbroker, who immersed young Warren in the world of finance.

Nebraska, Buffett's home state, truly suffered during the Great Depression, and growing up in that time and place had a lifelong impact on him. Thrifty with his money, and always looking to earn more, Buffett worked on a paper route at age thirteen. And at age fourteen, he earned enough to file his first tax return.

Throughout his teen years, Buffett remained enterprising, selling magazines and stamps door-to-door, and still delivering newspapers. He also went into business for himself (along with a friend), accumulating $2,000 by age fifteen. His investments and personal savings continued to grow, and he was able to help pay his way through college.

Upon graduating from the University of Nebraska, Buffett applied to Harvard Business School, and was rejected.

That turned out to be serendipitous. While instead attending prestigious Columbia University in New York, Buffett had the good fortune to learn from one of the keenest investing minds in the country, Benjamin Graham. From Graham, young Buffett learned about the principles of value investing, and he absorbed a key message: Every company has an innate value that's separate from its prevailing share price. He came away with his signature strategy, buying shares in companies that were worth intrinsically more than their stock prices suggested, companies that were undervalued by the market.

Soon after completing his college education, he started the Buffett Partnership, which eventually evolved into today's Berkshire Hathaway, to employ his investment philosophy. In fact, his first enormously successful investment was in Berkshire Hathaway, then a successful New England textile company, now one of the world's largest conglomerates. Today, Berkshire Hathaway acts as a holding company with many subsidiaries, including such well-known companies as:

- Benjamin Moore
- GEICO
- Dairy Queen
- Fruit of the Loom
- Pampered Chef
- Duracell
- Orange Julius
- Brooks Sports

In addition to those subsidiaries, Berkshire Hathaway has holdings in many more companies (including corporate giants like Capital One Financial Corp., General Motors, and Kraft Heinz). He is so successful that even jaded Wall Street insiders wait on tenterhooks to see what Warren Buffett will buy or sell next.

BENJAMIN GRAHAM

Financial security was the driving force behind Benjamin Graham's success. Born from his family's struggles after his father died when Benjamin was just nine years old, the now-renowned investor dedicated his professional life to financial stability.

His Wall Street career began in 1914, when Graham joined an investment firm with a job as a messenger. Within six short years,

Graham became a partner in the firm. Soon after that, he struck out on his own.

Reputedly personally wiped out by the market crash of 1929, Graham's investment partnership weathered that storm and eventually restored its coffers. Until the doors were closed in 1956, Graham's company brought its clients 17% average annual returns.

A keen investment manager and respected financier, Graham devoted much of his career to educating others. He began lecturing at his alma mater, Columbia University, in 1926 and kept at that for thirty years. During that time, he published *The Intelligent Investor,* which still serves as must-read material for serious investors.

Graham established two key investing principles that served him and his students quite well:

1. Fundamental security analysis
2. Value investing

Graham put forth the idea that an investment, in order to be successful, must be worth more than its share price. That is, it must be a good value. He also believed strongly in analysis, and judged companies by their numbers: balance sheets, profit margins, debt loads, and cash flow, among other things.

At the time of his death in 1976, Graham left a legacy of guiding principles to help investors thoughtfully analyze every stock they buy.

GEORGE SOROS

Though famed hedge fund manager George Soros is best known—and most despised—for his role as a currency pirate, his actions affected financial markets all over the world, including the stock market. As a speculator, this investing titan places very big bets on which way he thinks the markets will move, a practice that brought him enormous gains and losses, and made him one of the richest investors ever. But he didn't start out that way.

Born in Budapest, Hungary, in 1930, Soros's early life was darkly colored by the horrors of World War II and its devastating aftermath. At the tender age of seventeen, Soros fled Hungary to escape Soviet occupation and the weight of communism, landing in England where he first became involved in the world of finance. When he moved to the United States in 1956, Soros dove headfirst into investment banking.

By 1973, he established Soros Fund Management, a hedge fund that would later evolve into the renowned Quantum Group of Funds, funds that achieved massive success. Under his aggressive, speculative investing style, the fund posted huge returns, said to have come to more than 30% a year for nearly thirty years, including two years of returns greater than 100% (literally more than doubling the funds' holdings).

What Exactly Is a Hedge Fund?

A hedge fund is a private investment partnership that uses aggressive and risky strategies in the hopes of scoring huge gains. Only wealthy accredited investors are allowed to participate in these funds, which can invest however they want to and in anything they want to as long as they keep investors informed.

Those unbelievable returns were a direct result of Soros's underlying investing philosophy, termed "reflexivity." The basic premise is this: Investors' behavior has a direct impact on market fundamentals, and it's their actions that create the booms and busts that Soros sees as opportunities.

His most famous, and most infamous, deal brought Soros a $1 billion gain in a single day, and nearly wiped out the Bank of England. It was September 1992, a time when the British pound was strong, and Soros decided to bet against it. He borrowed billions of pounds, which he proceeded to convert into German marks. When the British pound crumbled, Soros reconverted those German marks at the new much more favorable exchange rate, and was able to repay his debt based on that new lower value of the pound. The difference between the values of the mark and the pound on that fateful day of September 16, 1992, brought George Soros a more than $1 billion profit.

After that, Soros was feared by governments around the world; they were terrified that the ruthless speculator would fix on their currencies, and then bankrupt them. They were right: In 1997, he placed a similar bet on the Thai baht, and again prevailed. But not every gamble brought a win.

In addition to his currency killings, Soros invested heavily in the stock market. When he turned his attentions to a corporation, he bet big and fast, choosing stocks based on an ever-shifting combination of information and intuition. Sometimes his gambles paid off; other times he was faced with staggering losses. For example, Soros bet on the US stock market in 1987, and lost close to $300 million when it crashed.

Later in life, Soros turned his attention toward political activism and his vast fortune toward charity, creating the Open Society Foundation to forward his philanthropy. Through the foundation, George Soros has donated billions of dollars to causes all around the world.

THE WITCH OF WALL STREET

The life of Henrietta Howland Robinson Green, best known as Hetty Green, was drenched in rumor and scandal. Her odd nature and unusual dress—she almost always wore black, and wore her clothes until they became threadbare—led people to call her the Witch of Wall Street. But the combination of her keen investment insights and miserly habits (which earned her another derogatory nickname, Hetty the Hoarder) made Hetty Green one of the richest women who ever lived.

Born to a sickly heiress and a distant, merciless businessman in 1834, Hetty had a remarkable grasp of finance at a very young age. By age eight, she had already opened her own savings account. As a child, she read the financial section of the newspaper almost every day to her grandfather (he was virtually blind), all the while discussing investments in great detail. That education served Hetty in her role as bookkeeper for her father's business, which did nothing to ease their cold relationship. In fact, when her mother died, Hetty's father blocked her inheritance, forcing the young woman to wait for his passing. When he died in 1864, Hetty finally had access to her family legacy of more than $5 million.

A short time later, Hetty's rich aunt died. Hetty had been expecting another inheritance; she claimed that her aunt had promised to leave Hetty her fortune. When the will was read, though, Hetty received a minuscule portion of the estate, with the rest parceled out among doctors and caretakers, even some distant cousins. Hetty contested that will, and produced another. Extensive legal battles ensued, and accusations of forgery were tossed around. The particular judge that she blamed for these legal troubles didn't bank on Hetty's powerful vindictiveness. As soon as she was able, she used her considerable financial resources to have him removed from the Chicago district court. Eventually, Hetty was awarded $600,000 of her aunt's $2 million estate.

Not content with her current fortune, Hetty brought her new influx of cash to Wall Street, snapping up low-risk investments. When the market declined amid panic sell-offs, Hetty bought in, buying at rock-bottom prices. Panicked bankers would come to her for emergency loans, which she gave them, as long as they agreed to her high-interest terms. As soon as the market turned around, she would demand immediate repayment with interest, and unload her cheaply bought investments for huge gains.

During the Panic of 1907, the Witch of Wall Street made the move that cemented her fortune. Her keen investor's intuition told her the market was heavily overvalued, prompting her to sell the majority of her holdings and call in all outstanding loans. She was right. While bankers and investors desperately tried to claw their way out of the gaping market bottom brought on by that great panic, Hetty Green quietly sat with her now-liquid fortune. When the dust settled, she bought up bargain stocks left and right. She now also required physical collateral (like land) for new loans she made. Though some painted her as a vulture, Hetty helped keep New York City solvent during that Panic, as their lender of last resort.

On the other side of the Hetty Green equation stood her near-pathological frugality. Despite her vast riches, Hetty moved around frequently, from one small apartment to the next, to get out of paying district taxes. One of the most heartbreaking examples of her miserly ways cost Ned, her only son, his leg. When the boy injured his leg, she brought him to a charity hospital to take advantage of their free care. His wound wasn't treated properly and became gangrenous, eventually leading to amputation, and replacement with a cork leg.

When finally she died in 1916, Hetty Green left a $100 million liquid legacy, allegedly accompanied by even more wealth left in holdings that did not bear her name.

CARL ICAHN

Hostile takeover king Carl Icahn had a knack for making corporate executives tremble in fear once he set his sights on their companies. But he didn't start out as a corporate raider.

Carl Icahn grew up in a middle-class family in Queens, New York. He went to Princeton on scholarship, dabbling in philosophy and medicine (until he realized that he hated working with corpses). In 1961, he got an entry-level job as a stockbroker, and quickly outgrew it. By 1968, Icahn had bought his own seat on the NYSE. And by the late 1970s, he kicked off his career as a corporate raider.

His most dubious claim to fame: Carl Icahn inspired the creation of more new SEC regulations than any other person in history, particularly in the area of disclosure rules. One of the original corporate raiders, Icahn cemented his position in Wall Street lore by hijacking TWA in a hostile takeover.

A financial bulldog, Icahn is known for scooping up majority positions in corporations, and then forcing the management to make profound changes designed to increase the stock price.

The ultimate corporate raider, Icahn continues to take over unwary corporations, and wield enormous financial clout.

JESSE LIVERMORE

Jesse Livermore lived a true "rags to riches" story, though one that ended in overwhelming tragedy. Born in the town of South Acton, Massachusetts, in 1877, Livermore headed to Boston in his early teens, hoping to avoid a life as a farmer. It was there he first discovered stock trading. A natural risk-taker, Livermore made a fortune shorting stocks, making money while everyone else was losing. At the peak of his wealth in 1929, he was worth nearly $100 million. In between, he made and lost several fortunes. Torn by the financial ups and downs, he took his own life in 1940.

Before his ill-fated death, though, Livermore was one of the most celebrated investors of his time. With no financial background, experience, or education, Jesse Livermore learned from his own market wins and losses. His career began when he was just a teenager, working in Boston as a chalk boy for Paine Webber, posting stock prices in the office.

Livermore dove headfirst into the stock market, raking in big money by the time he was fifteen: Rumor has it that he earned more than $1,000 in gains that year, a fortune in those days. Livermore earned a lot of his wealth by wagering against bucket shops, where all the action was based on stock price movements rather than stock trades. He was so successful that the Boston shops eventually banned him, spurring his move to New York City.

Decades before a click of the mouse brought up detailed price charts, graphs, and market news, Livermore's system involved gathering up available information and keeping track of stock prices and patterns in a handwritten ledger. His key strategy was to buy and sell stocks that were on the move. Once his stock target was selected, he watched for pivotal price points so as to carefully time his trades.

With his speculative style and focus on market directions, Livermore enjoyed staggering wins and demoralizing losses, and investors around the world eagerly anticipated his next moves.

DAVID DREMAN

Canadian David Dreman may not spark the same recognition as some of these other famed investors, but he perfected an investment strategy that has been followed successfully by many others: contrarian investing.

After losing a shocking amount of money in the late 1960s, and watching his wealth plummet by nearly 75%, Dreman learned the hard way that following the investing crowd was a surefire way to get burned. With that demoralizing experience behind him, Dreman began to look at the market in a whole new way, through the lens of investor psychology. That inspired his new contrarian investment philosophy, which boils down to "do the opposite."

Essentially, Dreman began investing against prevailing market trends and crowd behavior. He believed that herd behavior skewed stock prices, leading to mispriced shares. If he could exploit that difference then he could profit. In practice, he bought poorly performing stocks, and sold stocks that were doing well. Unlike mainstream investors, Dreman would seek out-of-favor corporations, focusing on those with low price-to-earnings ratios, then watch them outperform the market over time. And by the late 1970s, he had turned his fortune around completely, setting a remarkable example for novice investors.

THOMAS ROWE PRICE JR.

Contrary to the prevailing wisdom of his time, the dismal days following the crash of 1929, Thomas Rowe Price Jr. didn't believe in jumping in and out of the stock market, following trends and cycles, and carefully timing stock purchases and sales. Instead, he looked for solid companies, corporations that he expected big things from in the future. Not surprisingly, with that aim in mind, Price was dubbed the "father of growth investing."

Despite growing up during the Depression, and beginning his career in the shadow of the crash of 1929, Price tackled the stock market head-on, but in a manner very different than that of his contemporaries. Price studied companies, researched them, and bought for the long haul, an unpopular philosophy at the time. Dubbed "iron-willed" and tough to work with, Price's views were met with stony resistance from his bosses at the Baltimore firm Mackubin, Goodrich & Co. When the company decided to get rid of his department, Price left.

In 1937, Price struck out on his own, founding Price Associates, which has evolved into T. Rowe Price. He continued to work in his own distinct style, one we take for granted today but that didn't really exist before Price introduced it. Namely, he insisted on putting his clients' interests ahead of his firm's. To demonstrate his commitment, Price challenged the usual practices and set a new standard by charging client fees based on their holdings, and not charging commissions. In another landmark move, Price offered investment advice and counseling to his clients, something virtually unheard of at the time.

At the same time, he was fine-tuning his stock-picking methodology, focusing on the qualities he believed indicated superior long-term potential. Before investing in a corporation's stock, for example, an analyst from Price's company would meet with and interview the corporation's president. With his innovative system perfected, Price launched his company's first mutual fund, the T. Rowe Price Growth Stock Fund, back in 1950.

After decades of helping investors build their wealth, Price retired in the 1960s, and then sold off his interests in the firm that still bears his name.

JOHN TEMPLETON

Though his life began humbly in Winchester, Tennessee, John Templeton ended his days a billionaire. Born to a poor family in 1912, Templeton drove himself hard to succeed. He earned a scholarship to Yale, earning a degree in economics, and went on to earn a master's degree from Oxford University in England.

Just a few years later, in the midst of the Great Depression, the motivated young man (with a few partners) began an investment firm, which became enormously successful over the years, eventually growing into a $300 million business.

His dogged strategy, which he called bargain hunting, contributed to his wild success. In a classic, famous move, Templeton bought a $100 stake in every company whose stock was trading for less than $1. His investments in those 104 companies, some of which were actually bankrupt, roughly quadrupled in value in just four years' time. And he followed that strategy going forward, seeking out inexpensive companies of value that no one else was even looking at.

In 1954, Templeton launched the Templeton Growth Fund, his first mutual fund (a mutual fund is a big pool of money paid into by loads of investors so they can invest in a large, diverse portfolio of securities). Throughout his career, he established some of the most successful mutual funds in the world. In fact, his Templeton Growth Fund had astounding average annual returns of 13.8% over a fifty-year period.

JAMES "JUBILEE JIM" FISK

Jubilee Jim Fisk was murdered in a posh Manhattan hotel room in January 1872. The infamously unethical businessman had been involved in a scandalous love affair with actress Josie Mansfield, and the couple's notoriety saw them splashed all over the front pages. When the showgirl got together with frustrated businessman Edward Stokes to blackmail Fisk, Jubilee Jim resisted, and Stokes ended Fisk's life with a bullet. As huge as the man himself, Fisk's funeral involved a state militia unit and a 200-piece band.

Fisk's life was as scandalous and storied as his death. He was born in Bennington, Vermont, in 1835, but young Jim quickly moved on to splashier surroundings. His early work involved stints as a waiter, a salesman, a peddler, a smuggler, and a circus performer. Eventually, Fisk became a stockbroker, and that is where his path collided with the much-despised robber baron Jay Gould. Once the money started rolling in, Jubilee Jim loved to throw it around, and he spent quite a bit of it on the New York nightlife scene. Among other interests, Fisk bought the Grand Opera House and several other theaters in the city.

Easily recognizable with his heavy build and handlebar mustache, Fisk was well known for his unscrupulous Wall Street business tactics, and he was intimately involved in schemes that caused financial panics and wild market swings. At times, Fisk partnered up with notorious robber barons to make his cutthroat moves. But most often his partner was the secretive, surly Jay Gould.

JASON "JAY" GOULD

Being declared the most hated man in America did not bother Jason "Jay" Gould in the slightest. In fact, he thrived on the animosity, scorning his detractors. He made his Wall Street mark through manipulation, piracy, bribery, blackmail, and strikebreaking. The unsavory Gould prided himself on purposely running businesses into the ground, then rebuilding them for his own benefit.

Gould was a sickly child, born to an impoverished family in rural upstate New York in 1836. Not suited for farming, he turned to other trades, working as a blacksmith, a tanner, a surveyor, and a leather merchant before he finally became a stockbroker. In this capacity, the railroad industry caught his eye, and it led to one of the most infamous stock market wars in American history.

When he and Cornelius Vanderbilt battled over control of the Erie Railroad in 1867, Gould pulled every dirty trick he could muster. As Vanderbilt continued to secure shares in the company, Gould (along with Jim Fisk and Daniel Drew) illegally issued more than $5 million in new stock, watering down Vanderbilt's holdings. In an attempt to avoid arrest, Gould snuck out of New York and into New Jersey, where he quickly set up a new headquarters. To keep the industrious Vanderbilt out of his financial records (Vanderbilt had reportedly sent goons to grab them), Gould set three cannons along the Jersey City waterfront and launched a mini-fleet of small boats stocked with armed men into the water. When the law caught up with Gould, he had the law changed by bribing New York legislators in

Albany, making his once-illegal stock issue perfectly legal. In the end, Vanderbilt admitted defeat, leaving the Erie Railroad in the hands of Gould, Fisk, and Drew.

But the scintillating story of the Erie Railroad doesn't end there. Fisk and Gould forced Drew out of the railroad. A short time later, Fisk was murdered by his ex-girlfriend's new lover. That left Gould with their full shares of the Erie, until he was out-swindled by a man known as Lord Gordon-Gordon. Gould, in all his greed, wanted full control of the Erie Railroad, so he started to pull together cash and investors in order to buy up every share he could. Enter Gordon-Gordon, a Scottish "investor," who ensnared Gould in an elaborate web of lies. Gordon-Gordon convinced Gould that he could bring in even more aristocratic investors, and Gould responded by gifting the "lord" with nearly $1 million in Erie Railroad stock, which he turned around and sold immediately, funding his escape to Canada.

By 1879, Gould no longer had a stake in the Erie. Instead, he headed west, and set his sights on other growing railroads, including the Union Pacific.

Unlike many other affluent businessmen of his time, Gould never gave a dime of his vast fortune to charity. Despite his well-deserved reputation as a ruthless robber baron, Gould actually had some very positive effects on American society. Among those accomplishments, Gould was instrumental in forging a national railroad, as well as bringing Western Union to the top of the telegraph industry.

HISTORY'S BIGGEST SCAMS

Unleashing Tsunamis on Wall Street

Insider trading is one of the most widely known problems policed by the SEC, but it's not the only way investors can be scammed by corporations or their employees. While the SEC and reputable, honest public accounting firms work tirelessly to uncover frauds, a lot of schemes slip through, bilking shareholders out of millions—even billions—of dollars. And though corporate scams make for splashy headlines, a good story does nothing to help investors recoup their losses.

BERNARD MADOFF

By the time he was arrested, in 2008, Bernard Madoff had committed the single biggest fraud in the history of the US stock market: a $64.8 billion investment scam that duped thousands of sophisticated and institutional investors right along with SEC authorities. Though it's often said Madoff conned his investors to the point where their losses totaled $50 billion to $60 billion, that's not exactly accurate. Rather, they lost their original investments, totaling about $20 billion; the rest never really existed.

Madoff's scheme took root when he began to focus on automated trading systems. He created one of the first computerized programs to match buyers and sellers, vastly improving trade efficiency at his firm.

By the early 1990s, Madoff had become a financial industry staple, even serving as head of the tech-oriented NASDAQ stock exchange for three years. Madoff's advice was sought after and trusted, and big-money investors flocked to his investment fund, ignoring what should have been bright red flags because of their faith in him. And he didn't accept just any investor; he actually turned away many would-be investors, which only made his fund seem more exclusive and attractive.

A Parade of Familiar Names

The Bernard Madoff story might not have caught fire as quickly if it hadn't been for the well-known swindled investors, including Hollywood icon Steven Spielberg, ubiquitous film and TV star Kevin Bacon, and infamous former New York governor Eliot Spitzer.

The money seemed too good to be true, and it was: Madoff's firm offered investors steady high returns from low-risk investments, the holy grail of investing because it's virtually impossible. But every year, investors were seeing steady returns of 10% to 13% even as the markets swung up and down. Madoff worked under a cloak of secrecy, often denying investors online access to their accounts, and clearing his own trades without oversight. And because of his close connections to SEC officials, no one looked into Madoff's firm until it was too late.

As it turned out, Madoff's investing genius was no more than a Ponzi scheme. Those high, reliable returns weren't real; they were simply funds from new investors paid out to those who'd bought in earlier. When it all collapsed, his investors were left with nothing. And though on June 29, 2009, Madoff was sentenced to 150 years in prison; that was little solace to investors who lost everything.

VOLKSWAGEN AND "DIESELGATE"

Back in 2005, Volkswagen engineers created a new "cleaner" diesel engine to meet new nitrous oxide standards. Only it didn't work. So, to cover up the failure, they modified the software to help the vehicles fraudulently pass emissions tests they would otherwise fail.

Fast-forward to 2014, when researchers alerted the Environmental Protection Agency (EPA) and the California Air Resources Board (CARB) that there was a huge difference between test values and on-the-road nitrous oxide emissions. When they weren't in test mode, the diesel vehicles were emitting up to forty times more toxic fumes than company tests were showing. The discrepancy affected around 482,000 Volkswagen cars sold in the US and more than 10 million sold worldwide. The EPA began to investigate along with the US Department of Justice (DOJ).

By September 2015, Volkswagen stock took a huge hit, falling 30% when the news of its Clean Air Act violations hit. Months later, in January 2016, the DOJ and the EPA sued the corporation, resulting in a $14.7 billion settlement. That would include a $10 billion car buyback program along with money to fund projects to reduce toxic emissions.

Both executives and engineers were arrested and charged, with some going to prison and paying huge fines. A "corporate compliance monitor," an independent individual who makes sure all settlement terms are being followed, was put in place at the company for three years to prevent additional fraud.

In 2019, the SEC filed a fraud complaint alleging that the corporation and its CEO Martin Winterkorn defrauded investors to the tune of $13 billion.

THERANOS

Imagine if getting blood work was fast and easy—just a few drops instead of a bunch of tubes. That was the promise of the "Edison" technology created and promoted by Theranos. But it was all a lie.

In 2003 at age 19, Elizabeth Holmes founded Theranos, a company that would revolutionize blood tests. Less blood needed, rapid results...it sounded like the invention of a lifetime. Her one-time professor from Stanford (where she had dropped out after one year) connected her with venture capitalists, and she raised $6 million. Theranos attracted big-name board members (like former Secretary of State George Shultz) and big-ticket investors (like Rupert Murdoch and Betsy DeVos).

By 2015, pharmacy giant Walgreens had partnered with Theranos, investing a reported $140 million, believing Holmes's promises. Holmes was suddenly everywhere: in the media, on the covers of *Forbes* and *Fortune*. Her company was then valued at $9 billion, and Holmes was flying high—even though she knew her blood tests didn't work.

When employees told Holmes and other senior personnel about the problems with Edison, they were ignored, then threatened with legal action. One of those employees reported Theranos's problems to the Centers for Medicare and Medicaid Services (CMS). Another talked with a *Wall Street Journal* reporter who broke the story in October 2015.

After the news came out, Walgreens halted their partnership with Theranos. CMS announced that Theranos's tests were endangering patients by providing incorrect results.

Though Theranos had not yet gone public, the company had defrauded its investors. In 2018, the SEC charged the company and its founder with fraud. That was followed by indictments from a federal grand jury. Holmes was found guilty and sentenced to more than eleven years in prison. And Theranos was liquidated in September 2018.

COMMON SCHEMES

Psst, **Buddy, Wanna Buy a Solid Gold Watch for $50?**

Creating false information about stocks is extremely easy to do. Virtually anyone with a laptop or a smartphone can create realistic-looking websites and press releases with just a few clicks and judicious copy-and-paste action. Phishing, smishing, and vishing schemes are rampant, and new twists appear faster than ever before. Unsuspecting investors get caught up in the hype and excitement generated by hucksters. But investors who know the tricks of this illegal trade can avoid getting sucked into these schemes.

BOILER ROOMS

When it comes to high-pressure sales tactics, the infamous "boiler rooms" dominate.

Set up in large, cheap offices, crowds of telemarketers randomly cold-call potential investors to bully them into buying specific stocks. These stock pushers work for commissions, and they work aggressively, hawking otherwise unheard-of companies with exaggerated and outright false information about skyrocketing sales, 1,000% returns, and other outrageous claims.

Most often, the shares they're selling trade on the pink sheets, where there are virtually no disclosure requirements, and very little regulation. That Wild West atmosphere suits their purposes perfectly, as many of these "advisors" have no financial or securities qualifications at all. What they do have are persuasive personalities and intimidation tactics, and a very strong grasp on emotional manipulation.

PUMP AND DUMP

Unscrupulous brokers often hype and promote companies they hold shares in, even though those companies have only minimal assets and not a lot of prospects for real success. These ruthless salesmen contact potential investors by phone and email, and post enticing messages on Internet bulletin boards, inflating the real value of the company and tagging it as "the next big thing."

With these pump-and-dump schemes, hard-selling wheeler-dealer brokers hype the stocks to thousands of people, making outrageous claims about the company that are wholly unsubstantiated by the facts. The companies they choose are typically micro caps, for which independent or verifiable information can be very hard to find.

With their high-pressure sales tactics, these brokers encourage investors to dive in, which sharply increases the trading volume and liquidity of the shares, and drives up the share price—the "pump." When the share price spikes, these brokers sell their shares—the "dump"—and cash in on that artificial price inflation, raking in profits for a company that is worth nearly nothing.

SHORT AND DISTORT

In bear markets, pump-and-dump schemes don't work all that well because investors are more wary. In times like those, a sort of opposite scheme goes into play: the short-and-distort scheme. Here, dishonest traders use short selling in an underhanded way to take advantage of naive investors.

This type of scam also involves stock price manipulation, but in the opposite direction. The traders bad-mouth their target stock, one for which they hold a short position, to drive down its price as far as possible.

These con artists play on investor fear and worry, already heightened by the bear market. For this scheme to work, they must appear trustworthy, and so they often pretend to be associated with trusted authorities like the SEC and FINRA. This is especially easy to do by email. They claim to be looking after the best interests of the investor, protecting them from the "corporate liars" who are directly tied to the company. They try to convince investors to sell their shares because the company can't be trusted or some scandal is about to break. They may even mention class action lawsuits (that don't really exist), all in an effort to get investors to sell and force the stock price to bottom out.

When it does, they swoop in and buy up the shares at ridiculously low prices, shares that they have shorted at much higher, true value prices.

POOP AND SCOOP

Another twist on the pump-and-dump scheme is known as the poop and scoop, which mixes elements of the classic pump-and-dump scam and its short-and-distort cousin.

To conduct this scam, a small group of investors (sometimes just one) try to send a stock price into a free fall by circulating negative false information about the corporation and spurring the rumor mill. All of that damaging publicity takes a heavy toll on the company's stock price, sparking a mad sell-off.

The poop-and-scoop scammers then buy up that stock at bargain basement prices. When the stock rebounds to its true value, these scammers sell, amassing large profits.

PONZI SCHEME

Ponzi schemes made the headlines again during the Bernard Madoff scandal, in what was one of the biggest and most costly scams in financial history.

The first well-known scheme of this kind was perpetrated by an Italian immigrant named Charles Ponzi back in the 1920s. After being involved in a few unsuccessful criminal ventures, Ponzi came upon the scam of his life. He got a letter from Spain that contained an international reply coupon (IRC), a special coupon that let the holder trade it in for a specific number of priority postage stamps in another country. Ponzi quickly figured out that he could profit by having people abroad buy low-cost IRCs, have the IRCs sent to him, exchange them for more expensive stamps in the United States, and then sell the stamps. Allegedly, on some of these stamp sales Ponzi earned returns of more than 400%.

Then Ponzi realized he could make even more money if he had investors, and his postage plan rapidly turned into a scam. He began using the money from new investors to pay false returns to previous investors. Ponzi attracted thousands of New Englanders by promising sky-high 50% to 100% returns in ninety days, a much more tempting return than the annual 5% they could earn on their savings accounts. At one point, he was said to make $250,000 in a single day. But the scheme finally unraveled when investors tried to claim their money.

By the time of his arrest (for more than eighty counts of mail fraud) on August 12, 1920, Charles Ponzi owed investors nearly $7 million.

A Ponzi scheme is any investment swindle where supposed returns are paid to existing investors with money taken in from new investors. The schemers rope in new investors with the promise of much higher than average returns, ostensibly from blockbuster money-making opportunities with very little downside risk. Early investors receive their promised returns as new money flows in, giving the appearance of real profits from a successful business venture.

But all Ponzi schemes are destined to collapse, as the path to new investors dries up, or as many early investors look to cash out.

RECOVERY ROOM

Recovery room schemes prey on investors who have already lost money to con artists. These scammers frequently pose as government agencies or charitable organizations to help victims get their money back. To begin that recovery work, they request payment from the victim to cover their fees, sometimes a percentage of the original amount lost. Once they receive payment, they disappear, and the investor is saddled with even bigger losses.

INDEX

Accounting. *See* Finances and math
Accounting (book) value, 211–12
Accredited investors, 65–66
Acquisitions. *See* Mergers and acquisitions
American Depository Receipts (ADRs), 124
Annual reports, 197–201
Bankruptcy and failure of companies, 102–3
Barbarians at the Gate (film), 166–68
Bear markets, 46–47
Bell and after the bell, 14
Black days, 60
Blue chips, 112–13
BMV (la Bolsa Mexicana de Valores), 36–37
Boiler rooms, 261–62
Book value, 211–12, 215
Brokers. *See* Stockbrokers
Bubbles, 48–53
  about: forecasting, 50; overview of, 48
  building, 48–49
  crypto, 53
  dot-com, 51
  housing, 51–53
Buffett, Warren, 94, 110, 228–29, 240–42
Bull markets, 44–46
Businesses, characteristics of great companies, 227–28. *See also* Finances and math; Management and ownership of companies; Mergers and acquisitions
Buying and selling stocks. *See also* Economic indicators; Finances and math; Management and ownership of companies; Stockbrokers
  about: advanced techniques, 194; good price barometer, 181; overview of, 175
  analyzing stocks, 177–78
  annual reports and, 197–201
  Buffett approach to success, 228–29. *See also* Buffett, Warren
  buying what you know, 175–76
  executing trades, 180–84
  getting facts, 176–77
  herd mentality and, 231
  investor psychology and, 230–32
  IPOs, 191–93
  knowing when to sell, 178–79
  knowing yourself and, 232
  limit orders, 182–83
  margin buying, 194
  market orders, 180–82
  selling short, 195–96
  stock tables and, 202–3
  stop orders (buy/sell), 183–84
  ticker symbols and, 204–7
  ticker tape and, 208–10
  time frame for orders, 181–82
Carnegie, Andrew, 234–36
China
  about: global marketplace and, 40; impact of, 34, 35, 41
  SEHK and, 34–35
  SSE and, 33–34
Chipotle Mexican Grill (CMG), 13
Circuit breakers, 47
Classes of stocks, 109–11
Coincident indicators, 71
Common stock, 104–5, 110, 205, 215
Crashes (of 1929, 1987, 2010, 2015, 2020), 54–58
Cryptocurrency
  about: overview and origins of, 143
  blockchain and, 143
  bubble, 53
  funds, 145–46
  NFTs and, 146

scam alerts, 146–47
stock market and, 144
stocks, investing in, 144–45
Cumulative preferred stock, 108
Cyclical stocks, 118
Dealer market, 22–23
Defensive stocks, 119–20
Deflation, 69
Disney, 95, 100–101
Dividend investment plans (DRIPS), 151–52
Dividends, 10, 88, 106, 107–8, 115–17, 137, 148–51, 225–26
Dot-com bubble, 51
The Dow, 74–77
about: explained, 74–77; sale of, 77
bear markets and, 46–47
bull markets and, 44–46
historical extremes, 19–20, 45, 55–58, 60
points, weights, and Divisor, 75–76
presidential politics and, 72
rise and fall over 116 years, 76–77
Dreman, David, 250
DRIPS (dividend investment plans), 151–52
Earnings per share (EPS) and earnings growth, 215–20. *See also* Price-to-earnings growth (PEG) ratio
Economic indicators, 68–72
GDP (gross domestic product), 71–72
hemlines, libraries, presidents, 72
inflation and deflation, 68–69
leading, lagging, coincident, 71
market trends, 70
stagflation, 43
EDGAR, 66–67
ESOPs, 174
Euronext, 20, 35–36
Exchange-traded funds (ETFs), 124, 133–37
Exxon and Mobil merger, 158
Exxon Valdez catastrophe, 12–13
Famous and infamous investors, 233–39. *See also* Scandals and schemes
about overview of, 233
Buffett, Warren, 94, 110, 228–29, 240–42
Carnegie, Andrew, 234–36
Dreman, David, 250
Fisk, James "Jubilee Jim," 253–54, 255
Gould, Jason "Jay," 253, 254–55
Graham, Benjamin, 241, 242–43
Green, Henrietta "Hetty" Howland Robinson, 246–48
Icahn, Carl, 102, 248
Livermore, Jesse, 249–50
Morgan, J.P., 233–34
Price, Thomas Rowe Jr., 251–52
Rockefeller, John D., 236–37
Soros, George, 243–45
Templeton, John, 252–53
Vanderbilt, Cornelius, 237–39, 254–55
Finances and math. *See also* Economic indicators
about: finding sector ratios, 222; overview of, 211; variations of ratios, 223
basics of investor math, 211–20
book value, 211–12, 215
earnings per share (EPS) and earnings growth, 215–20
financial/annual reports, 197–201
market value, 215–16
par value, 214
price-to-earnings (P/E) ratio, 221–23
price-to-earnings growth (PEG) ratio, 224
price volatility, 10, 213
profit margin, 212–13
total returns, 225–26

Financial planners, 190
FINRA (Financial Industry Regulatory Authority), 15, 132, 188–89. *See also* SEC (Securities and Exchange Commission)
Fisk, James "Jubilee Jim," 253–54, 255
Foreign exchanges. *See also* International markets
  about: overview of, 29–30; time differences and, 30
  Euronext, 20, 35–36
  London Stock Exchange (LSE), 31
  Mexican Stock Exchange (aka BMV, Bolsa Mexicana de Valores), 36–37
  Shanghai Stock Exchange (SSE), 33–34. *See also* China
  Tokyo Stock Exchange (TSE), 31–32
Forms 10-K, 10-Q, and 8-K, 64–65
FT Wilshire 5000 (FTW5000), 85
GDP (gross domestic product), 71–72
Global Depositary Receipts (GDRs), 124
Global marketplace, 40. *See also* Foreign exchanges; International markets
Golden parachutes, 172–73
Gould, Jason "Jay," 253, 254–55
Graham, Benjamin, 241, 242–43
Green, Henrietta "Hetty" Howland Robinson, 246–48
Greenmail, 170
Growth, earnings, 220. *See also* Price-to-earnings growth (PEG) ratio
Growth stocks, 116–17
Hamilton, Alexander, 7
Herd mentality, 231
Holmes, Elizabeth, 259–60
Hostile takeovers, 163–74
  Barbarians at the Gate example, 166–68
  corporate raiders, 165–66
  explained, 163–64
  greenmail and, 170
  knights of many colors, 168
  proxy fights and, 168
  shark repellant (ESOPs, golden parachutes, macaroni defense, poison pills), 170–74
  tender offers, 169–70
  Williams Act and, 164–65
Housing bubble, 51–53
Icahn, Carl, 102, 248
Income stocks, 115–16
Indexes. *See also* S&P 500; The Dow
  about, 73
  FT Wilshire 5000 (FTW5000), 85
  NASDAQ Composite, 80
  NASDAQ 100, 81–82
  Russell 2000, 83–84
Inflation, 68–69
International Continental Exchange (ICE) buying, 20, 35
International markets. *See also* Foreign exchanges
  China's impact, 41
  developed, emerging, and frontier markets, 122–23
  global marketplace and, 40
  impact on US stock market, 38–41
  international stocks and, 122–25
  multinational corporations (MNCs) and, 39–40
  risks investing in, 125
  ways to by foreign stocks, 123–25
Investor math. *See* Finances and math
Investor psychology, 230–32
IPOs, 191–93
Johnson, F. Ross, 166–68
Lagging indicators, 71
Large-cap stocks, 87–88
Leading indicators, 71
Limit orders, 182–83
Livermore, Jesse, 249–50
London Stock Exchange (LSE), 31
Macaroni defense, 173

Madoff, Bernard, 256–57, 264
Management and ownership of companies
bad CEOs, 100–101
CEO pay scale (salaries, bonuses, and stock), 97–99
failure, bankruptcy and, 102–3
great company characteristics and, 227–28
investing in a piece of a company, 94–96
management structure, 96–97
shareholders taking a stand, 101–2
top CEO salaries for 2022, 99
Margin buying, 194
Market capitalization, 86–91
about: evaluating, 104; mega-cap and nano-cap companies, 87; overview of, 86–87
large-cap stocks, 87–88
micro-cap stocks, 90–91
mid-cap stocks, 88–89
small-cap stocks, 89–90
Market cycles. *See also* Bubbles; Panics
about: overview of, 42
bear markets, 46–47
bull markets, 44–46
circuit breakers, 47
crashes (of 1929, 1987, 2010, 2015, 2020), 54–58
Dow setting new records, 45
secular markets (long-lasting), 42–44
Market orders, 180–82
Market trends, 70
Market value, 215–16
Mergers and acquisitions, 156–62. *See also* Hostile takeovers
about: overview of, 156
acquisitions, 159–60
Exxon and Mobil merger, 158
impact on shareholders, 158–60
mergers, 156–59
unsuccessful, reasons for, 161–62
Mexican Stock Exchange (aka BMV, Bolsa Mexicana de Valores), 36–37
Micro-cap stocks, 90–91
Mid-cap stocks, 88–89
Morgan, J.P., 233–34
Multinational corporations (MNCs), 39–40
Mutual funds, 124, 128–32, 145, 252–53
NASDAQ (National Association of Securities Dealers Automated Quotations), 21–24
dealer market, 22–23
deal example, 24
origins, focus, and evolution, 21–22
stock market and, 7
NASDAQ Composite index, 80
NASDAQ 100, 81–82
NFTs, 146
NYSE (New York Stock Exchange)
big events last four decades, 19–20
history and early days, 18–20
International Continental Exchange (ICE) buying, 20, 35
players and their functions, 17–18
seats on, 16–17
size of, as Big Board, 16, 17
stock market, Wall Street and, 7, 16
trading process and open outcry system, 17–18
Whitney scandal, 18–19
NYSE Euronext, 20, 35–36
OTC (over-the-counter) market, 25–28, 90, 206
OTC Pink, 26–28
Panics, 59–62
about: black days, 60; description of, 59–60
2008, 60–61
2020 (COVID-19), 61–62
2023 (Silicon Valley Bank), 62
Participating preferred stock, 107–8
Par value, 214

Penny stocks, 126–27
Pink Market, 26–28
Poison pills, 171–72
Politics, stock market and, 11, 72
Ponzi schemes, 264–65
Poop and scoop schemes, 263–64
Preferred stock, 106–8, 116, 205–6
Price, Thomas Rowe Jr., 251–52
Price-to-earnings (P/E) ratio, 221–23
Price-to-earnings growth (PEG) ratio, 224
Price volatility, 213
Primary market, 8–9
Profit margin, 212–13
Proxy fights, 168
Psychology, investor, 230–32
Pump and dump schemes, 262
Raiders. *See* Hostile takeovers
Ratios. *See* Finances and math
Recovery room schemes, 265
"Red herrings" and "dog and pony show," 193
REITS (real estate investment trusts), 138–42
Returns. *See* Finances and math
Reverse stock splits, 154–55
Rockefeller, John D., 236–37
Russell 2000, 83–84
S&P 500
  circuit breakers, 47
  crashes and, 57, 58
  history and operations, 78–79
  together with the Dow, 77
Scandals and schemes. *See also* Famous and infamous investors
  about: biggest scams overview, 256; schemes overview, 261
  boiler rooms, 261–62
  Madoff, Bernard and, 256–57, 264
  Ponzi scheme, 264–65
  poop and scoop, 263–64
  pump and dump, 262
  recovery room, 265
  short and distort, 262–63
  stock market and examples, 11–13, 18–19
  Theranos and Elizabeth Holmes, 259–60
  Volkswagen emissions scandal, 13, 258
SEC (Securities and Exchange Commission), 63–67
  accredited investors and, 65–66
  EDGAR and, 66–67
  FINRA and, 15. *See also* FINRA (Financial Industry Regulatory Authority)
  Forms 10-K, 10-Q, and 8-K, 64–65
  origin and function, 63
Secondary market, 8, 9
Sectors, market, 92–93
Secular markets, 42–44
Self, knowing, 232
Shanghai Stock Exchange (SSE), 33–34
Shark repellant (ESOPs, golden parachutes, macaroni defense, poison pills), 170–74
Short and distort schemes, 262–63
Short sales, 195–96
Small-cap stocks, 89–90
Soros, George, 243–45
Splits, stock, 153–55
SSE (Shanghai Stock Exchange), 33–34
Stockbrokers
  about: overview of functions and using, 185
  discount brokers, 185–86
  dishonest, protecting yourself, 189–90
  financial planners and, 190
  full-service brokers, 186–88
  monitoring, 188–89
Stock market. *See also* Market cycles
  about: always moving, 7; this book and, 5–6

bell and after the bell, 14
corporate scandals and, 11–13
crypto and, 144–45
FINRA oversight, 15, 132, 188–89
international. *See* Foreign exchanges; International markets
market capitalization (large-cap to micro-cap), 86–91
mutual funds affecting, 132
origins and major institutions, 7–8
panics. *See* Panics
politics and, 11, 72
primary market, 8–9
SEC and. *See* SEC (Securities and Exchange Commission)
secondary market, 8, 9
sectors, 92–93
Stocks. *See also* Buying and selling stocks
about: overview of categories of, 104–5
appeal/benefits of, 9–10
blue chips, 112–13
cash benefit of, 10
classes of, 109–11
common stock, 104–5, 110, 205, 215
company ownership, management and, 94–103
cyclical stocks, 118
defensive stocks, 119–20
dividends, 10, 88, 106, 107–8, 115–17, 137, 148–51, 225–26
ETFs and, 124, 133–37
growth stocks, 116–17
income stocks, 115–16
international stocks, 122–25
investing in a piece of a company with, 94–96
long-term returns, 9–10
market sectors, 92–93
mutual funds, 124, 128–32, 145, 252–53
penny stocks, 126–27
preferred stock, 106–8, 116, 205–6
splits, 153–55
tech stocks, 121
ticker symbols, 204–7
value stocks, 114–15
volatility of, 10, 213
Stock tables, 202–3
Stop orders (buy/sell), 183–84
Super shares, 109–10
Symbols, stock ticker, 204–7
Tables, stock, 202–3
Taxes, 116, 125, 137, 152
Tech stocks, 121
Templeton, John, 252–53
Tender offers, 169–70
Theranos and Elizabeth Holmes, 259–60
Ticker symbols, 204–7
Ticker tape, 208–10
Tokyo Stock Exchange (TSE), 31–32
Tokyo Stock Price Index (TOPIX), 32
Total returns, 225–26
Tylenol scare, 12
Underwriters, 191
Values. *See* Financial planners
Value stocks, 114–15
Vanderbilt, Cornelius, 237–39, 254–55
Volatility, price, 10, 213
Volkswagen emissions scandal, 13, 258
Websites, corporate, 212
Williams Act, 164–65

ABOUT THE AUTHOR

Michele Cagan is a CPA, author, and financial mentor. With more than twenty years of experience, she offers unique insights into personal finances, from breaking out of debt and minimizing taxes to maximizing income and building wealth. Michele has written numerous articles and books about small business finances, investing, and accounting, including *The Infographic Guide to Personal Finance, Real Estate Investing 101, Investing 101, Budgeting 101,* and *The Financial Recovery Workbook.* In addition to her financial know-how, Michele has a not-so-secret love of painting, Star Wars, and chocolate. She lives in Maryland with her kid, dogs, cats, and koi. Get more financial guidance from Michele by visiting MicheleCaganCPA.com.